POWER FOR ALL

The Baptism in the Holy Spirit

and

Speaking in Tongues

Bill and Eva Dooley

Updated Edition

POWER FOR ALL
The Baptism in the Holy Spirit
and
Speaking in Tongues

Updated Edition

Printed in the United States of America
Bill and Eva Dooley
BillandEvaDooley.com

The authors have taken the liberty of using *italics* for Scripture quotations. In some passages, the use of quotation marks has been simplified and final punctuation has been standardized. Otherwise, punctuation and capitalization reflect the usage of the version cited. Certain words and phrases within Scripture quotations have been highlighted in **boldface** print for emphasis.

ACKNOWLEDGMENTS

Our sincere thanks...

To our heavenly Father for giving us His Son, Jesus Christ, and for blessing us with His precious Holy Spirit.

To those who have enriched us through the years with books, teachings, and testimony on the Person and ministry of the Holy Spirit. The list of names would be too long to include here.

To our beloved daughter, Dr. Christina Dooley, who has devoted countless hours to reviewing this book and making numerous editorial and biblical suggestions for its completion.

To our gifted brother-in-law, John Pearson, for the many hours he spent typing the manuscript and giving valuable input.

May you all be abundantly rewarded for your dedication and participation.

CONTENTS

PREFACE

The Holy Bible has much to say about the Person and ministry of the Holy Spirit, and many books have been written about Him, so we did not set out to write yet another book. However, as we have ministered to people over the years, in both individual and group settings, we have seen a need to make available the various Scriptures on the baptism in the Holy Spirit. Often, after praying for people to receive the baptism in the Holy Spirit, we would write down on a piece of paper some of the Bible verses for them to study when they got home. Realizing the need for these Scriptures and for clear biblical explanations, we decided to compile this book as an instructional tool for those who want to know more about the Holy Spirit.

These are the "last days" and God is indeed pouring out His Spirit upon His people. We have had the privilege of seeing hundreds come into this experience, both in the States and in other countries. Sometimes this ministry is to just one individual and other times to large groups. We will always remember the time we were ministering at a church in Peru, up in the Andes mountains in the Sacred Valley of the Incas. The first night our team gave a salvation message, and many received Jesus that evening. Then the second night I shared about the Holy Spirit, with Bill at my side interpreting from English to Spanish. At the end of the message, we gave an invitation for those who desired to receive the Holy Spirit with the evidence of speaking in other tongues to stand up. To our great surprise, the entire congregation stood to their feet! We had to repeat the invitation to make sure that they had understood what we were saying, and to make sure they knew that the altar call was specifically for those who did not have that experience already. One lady and a small child sat down, but the rest remained standing. We found out later that the lady already had the experience. The Holy Spirit came down in a mighty way over that congregation that night, and they were all filled with the Holy Spirit and began to speak in other tongues. But they did not just receive a new language—they received God's mighty power. They were empowered to witness to others, and that congregation has grown both spiritually and numerically as a result.

A similar thing happened one evening at a church near Frankfurt, Germany. After we shared God's Word, an invitation was given for those who wanted to receive Jesus in their hearts to raise their hands. So many hands went up that I turned to the pastor who was interpreting for me and asked him to make sure that the invitation was clear, that it was only for those who had never prayed the prayer of salvation before. The pastor said to me, "These people are all new. I have never seen these people at my church before." They were all led to pray the prayer of salvation, and right after that the Lord directed us to ask how many wanted to receive the Holy Spirit and His power. The same people (and others who were already believers) were eager to have that experience as well. We had them come to the altar, and as they did, the Holy Spirit came down upon the group and they began to pray in other tongues. As the awesome power of our Lord was touching them, many experienced different manifestations, including tears, laughter, physical or emotional healing, and other breakthroughs. People were saved, filled with the Spirit, and set free by the power of God—all in one meeting.

This power is for all who love Jesus and want more of His Spirit. Our heavenly Father is multigenerational, and at times He has poured out His Spirit upon entire families. No one is too old or too young to have this experience. And nothing touches our hearts more than to see little children being baptized in the Holy Spirit.

We remember how an eight-year-old boy in West Texas described his experience. On his own, he had responded to the altar call and joined the grownups who had come to receive the Holy Spirit at the front of the church. After he was prayed for and the Lord touched him, he ran to the back of the church where his mother was sitting with two other little boys. He proceeded to tell his mother, "Mom, the Holy Spirit came in here (pointing to his belly) like an airplane—zoom!" Those big planes have powerful engines, and this eight-year-old had felt God's power come into him like a powerful airplane. Jesus said, "But you shall receive power when the Holy Spirit has come upon you..." (Acts 1:8). Then that young boy took hold of the other two little boys that were sitting with his mother and brought them to the altar. He wanted them to have what he had just received, and they were also blessed.

I could go on and on sharing testimonies of people who have been touched and changed by the power of the Holy Spirit. Each experience is unique, because God ministers to each of us in a personal way. Bill and I know that firsthand. When we came into this spiritual experience back in 1975, we each had to respond and receive in an individual way. We had both been raised in Christian homes, and from an early age we knew and loved Jesus. Bill's parents, who had been in church leadership, had warned him to stay away from "tongue talkers" because they did not believe that "tongues" were of God. I had come from a devout liturgical church that included in the yearly calendar of Scripture readings the Pentecostal experience from Acts 2, but I did not realize that the power of the Holy Spirit was also for us. Needless to say, when the Lord began to give us fresh revelation that this experience is for all Christians in all places at all times, we had to overcome the old mindsets of tradition and the doctrines of men, and seek to know the truth from the Word of God. The more we read the Scriptures, the more convinced we became that this experience was for us, and we both were hungry to have all that our loving heavenly Father had for us. It was a miracle how He prepared our hearts. He enabled us to overcome our fears, questions, and concerns about how our family and friends would react to our decision to pursue more of God's Spirit.

It was our love for the Lord and our hunger for more of Him that propelled us forward, ready to receive all that He had for us. At that time we were members of a Methodist church, and we were very committed and involved in serving in that church. But when some friends invited us one evening to go with them to a special service at a different church where they were having revival meetings that week, we were more than happy to accept their invitation. At the end of that service, the guest speaker invited all those who wanted the baptism in the Holy Spirit to come forward, and we both found ourselves at the altar. The Lord ministered to us in unique and personal ways, and our lives have never been the same since. It's like our Christian walk took on a deeper dimension. Our love for the Lord was stronger. Our Bible reading, our understanding of God's Word, and our prayer life all intensified. We had more joy and more concern for our fellow man. We wanted everyone to come into this glorious life.

This is indeed a major purpose of the baptism in the Holy Spirit. As Jesus said in Acts 1:8, it is to give us the power to be His witnesses, far and near. And this is what He has empowered us to do, opening doors for us to go to many places in the States and other nations to share His Word and to minister. As a result of that empowerment, we have seen an increase of both the fruit of the Spirit and the gifts of the Spirit in our lives.

If you have a relationship with Jesus, the Holy Spirit is already present in your life, but there is more for you. On the other hand, if you have never asked Jesus to come into your heart by faith, the Holy Spirit will reveal Jesus to you and lead you to Him. If you have received the baptism in the Holy Spirit, you still need to be continually filled (Ephesians 5:18). Regardless of where we are now in our spiritual journeys, we all need more of the Holy Spirit. We need to know Him personally. We need to experience His sweet fellowship and His mighty power.

It is our prayer that as you read this book, the Scriptures will come alive to you, and you will come to know the Holy Spirit and experience His power in your life. As you come to know more about the Holy Spirit, you will know more about Jesus, for the Holy Spirit testifies of Jesus and glorifies Him (John 15:26; 16:14-15). And as you know more about Jesus, you will know more about the heavenly Father, for Jesus said that whoever has seen Him has seen the Father (John 14:9).

Eva Dooley

TO THE READER

The very fact that you now hold this book in your hand means that God has led you to this step in your spiritual journey with Him. Our heavenly Father has been at work, purposely using the events of your life to draw you closer to Himself. There is a hunger within you for more of the Lord, and He is the only One who can satisfy it. His wonderful promise to you is, "Blessed are those who hunger and thirst for righteousness, for they shall be filled" (Matthew 5:6).

Having grown up in the sixties, I can still remember the popular song that asked, "Is that all there is?" I can very confidently answer: "No, there is something more!" There is a whole dimension of power that many Christians have not yet come into, or have not fully experienced. It's the infilling of the Holy Spirit. This added dimension is not a secret. It's in God's book, the Bible, ready for all to discover.

As Jesus Christ was preparing His original disciples to go forth and evangelize the world, He knew that they would need something more. Those disciples knew the Lord. They had been trained and involved in the ministry, but they needed the supernatural power of the Holy Spirit to enable them to carry out their challenging task. For this reason, as part of the Great Commission, Jesus commanded them to wait in Jerusalem for the Holy Spirit to come and empower them (Luke 24:49).

When this happened, it was not some vague mystical awareness that settled over the disciples like an ethereal mist. They were filled with the power of God's Spirit.

This was a specific supernatural experience, which is called “the baptism in the Holy Spirit.” And this was not a one-time miracle that happened only to the disciples of old; it is a very real experience that continues to bless and transform believers even today.

It is our sincere hope that this book will increase your hunger for the Lord and lead you, as a modern disciple, into this glorious spiritual experience. Like salvation, the baptism in the Holy Spirit is a life-changing encounter with the Lord. In the words of Jesus Himself, “But you shall receive power when the Holy Spirit has come upon you...” (Acts 1:8). You will never be the same.

Bill Dooley

POWER FOR ALL

THE HOLY SPIRIT AND HIS INVALUABLE MINISTRY

The Holy Spirit is God. He is a vital Member of the Holy Trinity. He is God in action—the very power of God. He is the spiritual presence of Jesus in the world today. Since He is God's Spirit on earth, the Holy Spirit interrelates with us and enables us to experience God personally. In addition to His activity today, the Spirit of God was powerfully at work in both the Old and New Testaments.

The Holy Spirit in the Old Testament

As we read the Old Testament, we find that the Holy Spirit came upon different individuals on special occasions to enable them to accomplish certain tasks, but generally He did not remain upon them all the time.

One of those individuals was Samson. The Spirit of God came upon him, and he had supernatural strength to defeat the enemies of Israel:

> Judges 15:14-15
> 14 *When he came to Lehi, the Philistines came shouting against him. Then* ***the Spirit of the LORD came mightily upon him****; and the ropes that were on his arms became like flax that is burned with fire, and his bonds broke loose from his hands.*
> 15 *He found a fresh jawbone of a donkey, reached out his hand and took it, and killed a thousand men with it.*

We also read that the Spirit of God came upon Gideon and empowered him to lead Israel to defeat the Midianites:

Judges 6:34
But ***the Spirit of the LORD came upon Gideon****; then he blew the trumpet, and the Abiezrites gathered behind him.*

Other leaders, like Saul and David, were anointed by the Holy Spirit to lead God's people.

King Saul was empowered by the Holy Spirit, and on one occasion the prophetic anointing came upon him when he connected with a group of prophets, and he also started prophesying:

1 Samuel 10:1, 6, 9-10 (NIV)
1 *Then Samuel took a flask of oil and poured it on Saul's head and kissed him, saying, "Has not the LORD anointed you leader over his inheritance?*
6 ***The Spirit of the LORD will come upon you in power****, and you will prophesy with them; and you will be changed into a different person."*
9 *As Saul turned to leave Samuel, God changed Saul's heart, and all these signs were fulfilled that day.*
10 *When they arrived at Gibeah, a procession of prophets met him;* ***the Spirit of God came upon him in power****, and he joined in their prophesying.*

David was another man anointed by the Holy Spirit through Samuel:

1 Samuel 16:13 (NIV)
So Samuel took the horn of oil and anointed him in the presence of his brothers, and from that day on ***the Spirit of the LORD came upon David in power****...*

It was also the Holy Spirit who empowered and inspired the various prophets to speak on behalf of the Lord:

Micah 3:8 (NIV)
*But as for me, I am filled with **power, with the Spirit of the LORD**, and with justice and might, to declare to Jacob his transgression, to Israel his sin.*

In the Old Testament, before Adam and Eve sinned, God walked and talked with them in the Garden of Eden. Then the curse of sin put a barrier between God and man, but God never abandoned His people. He continued to intervene in the earth through His Spirit, and at times appeared to people (Genesis 12:7; 26:2; Numbers 20:6).

In the New Testament, the broken fellowship between God and man was restored by Christ's atoning death and resurrection, allowing God's constant presence through the Holy Spirit and the infilling of His power.

The Holy Spirit in the New Testament

There are some important distinctions between the ways that God related to His people in the Old Testament and how He relates to believers in the New Testament.

When Jesus died on the cross and rose from the dead, the price was paid for sin for anyone believing in and accepting Him as Savior. When someone receives Jesus, the Spirit of God comes to live in him. In both the Old and New Testaments God is **for** and **with** His people, but in the New Testament we find that the Lord dwells **in** His people by the Holy Spirit:

1 Corinthians 3:16
*Do you not know that you are the temple of God and that the **Spirit of God dwells in you**?*

This passage says that it is the "Spirit of God" that lives within believers. The phrase "Spirit of God" includes all three Persons of the Trinity. In all of our emphasis on the Holy Spirit in this study, we in no way wish to exalt the Holy Spirit above Jesus or the Father. The Holy Spirit brings glory to Jesus, and not to Himself:

John 15:26
"But when the Helper comes, whom I shall send to you from the Father, the Spirit of truth who proceeds from the Father, ***He will testify of Me****."*

John 16:13-14 (NIV)
13 *"But when he, the Spirit of truth, comes, he will guide you into all truth. He will not speak on his own; he will speak only what he hears, and he will tell you what is yet to come.*
14 ***He will bring glory to me*** *by taking from what is mine and making it known to you."*

So when we say that the Holy Spirit indwells a person, we are saying that God (the Father, the Son, and the Holy Spirit) lives in that person—the three are one:

1 John 4:15
Whoever confesses that Jesus is the Son of God, ***God abides in him****, and he in God.*

John 14:23
Jesus answered and said to him, "If anyone loves Me, he will keep My word; and My Father will love him, and ***We will come to him and make Our home with him****."*

There are passages that say that God inhabits His people, and others say that Jesus and the Holy Spirit do. These verses are not contradictory, but rather complementary:

Romans 8:9-11
9 *But you are not in the flesh but in the Spirit, if indeed* ***the Spirit of God dwells in you****. Now if anyone does not have* ***the Spirit of Christ****, he is not His.*
10 *And* ***if Christ is in you****, the body is dead because of sin, but the Spirit is life because of righteousness.*
11 *But* ***if the Spirit of Him who raised Jesus from the dead dwells in you****, He who raised Christ from the dead will also give life to your mortal bodies through* ***His Spirit who dwells in you****.*

Here the Apostle Paul equates the Holy Spirit with the Spirit of God and the Spirit of Christ. All three Members of the Trinity indwell the believer.

We should keep in mind that although all three Persons of the Godhead—the Father, the Son, and the Holy Spirit—are involved in salvation, it is through Jesus that we are saved. The Holy Spirit brings about spiritual change, but Jesus is the Savior:

Acts 4:10-12
10 *"let it be known to you all, and to all the people of Israel, that by the* ***name of Jesus Christ*** *of Nazareth, whom you crucified, whom God raised from the dead, by Him this man stands here before you whole.*
11 *This is the 'stone which was rejected by you builders, which has become the chief cornerstone.'*
12 *Nor is there salvation in any other, for there is* ***no other name*** *under heaven given among men by which we must be saved."*

John 20:31
but these are written that you may believe that Jesus is the Christ, the Son of God, and that ***believing you may have life in His name****.*

Another significant difference in the New Testament is that the Holy Spirit indwells **all** who receive Jesus as their Savior:

> 1 Corinthians 12:13
> *For by one Spirit we were all baptized into one body—whether Jews or Greeks, whether slaves or free—and have* ***all*** *been made to drink into one Spirit.*

In addition, in contrast with the way the Holy Spirit came upon individuals and then departed in the Old Testament, in the New Testament He remains within believers continually:

> John 14:16
> *"And I will pray the Father, and He will give you another Helper, that He may abide with you* ***forever****."*

We are blessed to have such an awesome Companion within us at all times. The Holy Spirit does many things **for** believers, **in** believers, and **through** believers. In the next section we will examine some of His attributes.

(1) The Holy Spirit is our Paraclete.

A Greek word often used in the New Testament to refer to the Holy Spirit is *paracletos,* rendered in English as "paraclete." It literally means one who is called alongside, implying one who is summoned to help.

There is a wealth of meaning in this word. It can be translated a number of ways: advocate, comforter, consoler, encourager, counselor, helper, exhorter, advisor, intercessor, strengthener, etc. Each of these meanings reveals an aspect of the ministry of the Holy Spirit.

The Greek text uses *paracletos* in John 14:16, 14:26, 15:26, and 16:7, but different versions of the Bible translate the word differently. For example, the King James Bible and some other versions translate it "Comforter," but others use "Helper" or "Counselor":

> John 14:16 (KJV)
> *"And I will pray the Father, and he shall give you another* ***Comforter****, that he may abide with you for ever."*
>
> John 14:16 (NKJV)
> *"And I will pray the Father, and He will give you another* ***Helper****, that He may abide with you forever."*
>
> John 14:16 (NIV)
> *"And I will ask the Father, and he will give you another* ***Counselor*** *to be with you forever."*

Here is how the Amplified Bible translates this same verse:

> John 14:16 (AMP)
> *"And I will ask the Father, and He will give you another Comforter (Counselor, Helper, Intercessor, Advocate, Strengthener, and Standby) that He may remain with you forever."*

The precious Holy Spirit is with us at all times and in all places. He comforts, helps, counsels, encourages, and strengthens us. Besides all these ministries, the Holy Spirit does even more. The following are some additional roles of the Holy Spirit.

(2) The Holy Spirit testifies of Jesus.

An important ministry of the Holy Spirit is to bear witness of Jesus. He speaks about Jesus and reveals the truth about Him:

> John 15:26
> *"But when the Helper comes, whom I shall send to you from the Father, the Spirit of truth who proceeds from the Father, He will **testify of Me**."*

The Holy Spirit does not call attention to Himself. He draws attention to Jesus.

(3) The Holy Spirit convicts us.

Another important role of the Holy Spirit is to convict individuals of sin and to lead them to repentance and conversion. It is He who brings us to Jesus the Savior:

> John 16:8
> *"And when He has come, He will **convict** the world of sin, and of righteousness, and of judgment."*

> 1 Corinthians 12:3
> *Therefore I make known to you that no one speaking by the Spirit of God calls Jesus accursed, and no one can say that Jesus is Lord except by the Holy Spirit.*

(4) The Holy Spirit gives us new life.

When we accept Jesus as Savior, the Holy Spirit makes us a new creation in Christ (2 Corinthians 5:17). He imparts spiritual life:

Ezekiel 36:26-27
26 *"I will give you a **new heart** and put a new spirit within you; I will take the heart of stone out of your flesh and give you a heart of flesh.*
27 *I will put My Spirit within you and cause you to walk in My statutes, and you will keep My judgments and do them."*

John 6:63
*"It is the Spirit who **gives life**..."*

John 3:5-6
5 *Jesus answered, "Most assuredly, I say to you, unless one is born of water and the Spirit, he cannot enter the kingdom of God.*
6 *That which is born of the flesh is flesh, and that which is **born of the Spirit** is spirit."*

Jesus spoke of spiritual rebirth as being "born again." The first birth is the natural one, but the new birth is the spiritual one. The process by which the Holy Spirit gives new life is called "regeneration":

John 3:3
*Jesus answered and said to him, "Most assuredly, I say to you, unless one is **born again**, he cannot see the kingdom of God."*

Titus 3:5
*not by works of righteousness which we have done, but according to His mercy He saved us, through the washing of **regeneration** and renewing of the Holy Spirit.*

The Holy Spirit quickens (makes alive) and revives:

Romans 8:11
But if the Spirit of Him who raised Jesus from the dead dwells in you, He who raised Christ from the dead will also ***give life*** *to your mortal bodies through His Spirit who dwells in you.*

(5) The Holy Spirit confirms our salvation.

He assures us that we are born again by giving us an inner knowledge in our spirit:

Romans 8:16
The Spirit Himself ***bears witness*** *with our spirit that we are children of God.*

(6) The Holy Spirit seals us.

In ancient Eastern tradition, a seal was placed on documents by someone in authority to authenticate them. Used figuratively here, the seal of the Lord assures us of His approval. God's mark is upon us, showing that we are His by the covenant in Christ's blood:

Ephesians 1:13 (NIV)
And you also were included in Christ when you heard the word of truth, the gospel of your salvation. Having believed, you were ***marked in him with a seal****, the promised Holy Spirit.*

Ephesians 4:30 (AMP)
And do not grieve the Holy Spirit of God [do not offend or vex or sadden Him], by Whom you were ***sealed*** *(marked, branded as God's own, secured) for the day of redemption (of final deliverance through Christ from evil and the consequences of sin).*

(7) The Holy Spirit guides us into truth.

John 16:13
"However when He, the Spirit of truth, has come, ***He will guide you into all truth****..."*

Jesus calls Him "the Spirit of truth":

John 15:26
"But when the Helper comes, whom I shall send to you from the Father, ***the Spirit of truth*** *who proceeds from the Father, He will testify of Me."*

(8) The Holy Spirit teaches us.

John 14:26
"But the Helper, the Holy Spirit, whom the Father will send in My name, ***He will teach*** *you all things, and bring to your remembrance all things that I said to you."*

Luke 12:12
"For the Holy Spirit will ***teach*** *you in that very hour what you ought to say."*

(9) The Holy Spirit reveals the future and God's divine plans.

John 16:12-13
12 *"I still have many things to say to you, but you cannot bear them now.*
13 *However, when He, the Spirit of truth, has come, He will guide you into all truth; for He will not speak on His own authority, but whatever He hears He will speak; and* ***He will tell you things to come****."*

1 Corinthians 2:9-11
9 *But as it is written: "Eye has not seen, nor ear heard, Nor have entered into the heart of man The things which God has prepared for those who love Him."*
10 *But God has* ***revealed*** *them to us through His Spirit. For the Spirit searches all things, yes, the deep things of God.*
11 *For what man knows the things of a man except the spirit of a man which is in him? Even so no one knows the things of God except the Spirit of God.*

(10) The Holy Spirit sets us free.

Romans 8:2
For the law of the Spirit of life in Christ Jesus has made me ***free*** *from the law of sin and death.*

2 Corinthians 3:17 (NIV)
Now the Lord is the Spirit, and where the Spirit of the Lord is, there is ***freedom****.*

(11) The Holy Spirit speaks to us.

John 16:13
"However, when He, the Spirit of truth, has come, He will guide you into all truth; for He will not ***speak*** *on His own authority, but whatever He hears He will* ***speak****; and He will* ***tell*** *you things to come."*

Acts 8:29
Then the Spirit ***said*** *to Philip, "Go near and overtake this chariot."*

Revelation 2:7
"He who has an ear, let him hear what the Spirit ***says*** *to the churches..."*

(12) The Holy Spirit leads us.

Romans 8:14
For as many as are ***led*** *by the Spirit of God, these are sons of God.*

(13) The Holy Spirit restrains us.

A major blessing that Christians have is the guidance of the Holy Spirit. He not only guides us to the right places, but at times He guides us away from the wrong places. When the Holy Spirit restrains us, He prevents us from doing something harmful or something against the will or timing of God. God knows best—He has the perfect plan. Sometimes He may say "No" and sometimes "No, not now." When the Lord tells us "No," and He prevents us from doing something, the timing may not be right.

This is what happened in Acts 16. Paul and his companions had planned to go minister in the province of Asia, but the Holy Spirit did not allow them. Then they decided to go to the region of Bithynia, but again they were not permitted. We do not know exactly how the Holy Spirit spoke to them—whether it was through a prophecy, a vision, an inner voice or circumstances—but the Holy Spirit stopped them from going to those places at that time:

Acts 16:6-7
6 *Now when they had gone through Phrygia and the*

> *region of Galatia, they* ***were forbidden*** *by the Holy Spirit to preach the word in Asia.*
> 7 *After they had come to Mysia, they tried to go into Bithynia, but the Spirit* ***did not permit them.***

Instead, the Holy Spirit directed them through a vision to go to Macedonia, where they were needed:

> Acts 16:8-10 (NIV)
> 8 *So they passed by Mysia and went down to Troas.*
> 9 *During the night Paul had a vision of a man of Macedonia standing and begging him, "Come over to Macedonia and help us."*
> 10 *After Paul had seen the vision, we got ready at once to leave for Macedonia, concluding that God had called us to preach the gospel to them.*

The Lord knew best where Paul and his companions were to go, and when. By the guidance of the Holy Spirit, they went to Europe instead. When the Spirit directed them to not go to the province of Asia, it was not a matter of denial, but delay. Paul did go there later, and many in that area received the Word and were converted (Acts 19:10). The Gospel also reached the region of Bithynia, and many there became Christians (1 Peter 1:1-2).

These men were led of the Lord, and they experienced phenomenal results. But let us hasten to point out that following the guidance of the Holy Spirit and being in the will of God does not guarantee that we will be free from trials and problems. Not long after Paul and Silas obediently went to Macedonia, they were beaten and thrown into prison (Acts 16:20-24).

It is during difficult times that we especially appreciate the presence and power of the Holy Spirit. These men were able to go through that painful experience without questioning or complaining. Instead, in spite of their circumstances, they were singing and worshiping God until midnight, when He caused an earthquake to set them free. As a result of their powerful witness, all the prisoners were blessed, and the jailer and his household were saved (Acts 16:16-34).

So if the Holy Spirit restrains us or changes our plans, we can trust that His ways and timing are perfect. When this is difficult for us to see and accept, His Word assures us that His thoughts are higher than ours (Isaiah 55:9).

(14) The Holy Spirit inspires us.

> 2 Timothy 3:16
> *All Scripture is given by* ***inspiration of God****, and is profitable for doctrine, for reproof, for correction, for instruction in righteousness.*
>
> 2 Peter 1:20-21 (TLB)
> *For no prophecy recorded in Scripture was ever thought up by the prophet himself. It was the Holy Spirit within these godly men who* ***gave them true messages from God****.*
>
> Job 32:8 (KJV)
> *But there is a spirit in man: and the* ***inspiration of the Almighty*** *giveth them understanding.*

(15) The Holy Spirit helps us pray.

When we do not know what to pray for or how, the Holy Spirit helps us and guides our prayer:

Romans 8:26-27
26 *Likewise the Spirit also helps in our weaknesses. For we do not know what we should pray for as we ought, but the Spirit Himself* ***makes intercession*** *for us with groanings which cannot be uttered.*
27 *Now He who searches the hearts knows what the mind of the Spirit is, because He* ***makes intercession*** *for the saints according to the will of God.*

(16) The Holy Spirit commissions us.

The Holy Spirit is involved in commissioning individuals for ministry. On one occasion, He spoke to the prophets and teachers of the church at Antioch to set apart Barnabas and Paul for the work God had for them:

Acts 13:2-4
2 *As they ministered to the Lord and fasted, the Holy Spirit said, "Now separate to Me Barnabas and Saul for the work to which I have called them."*
3 *Then, having fasted and prayed, and laid hands on them, they sent them away.*
4 *So, being sent out by the Holy Spirit, they went down to Seleucia, and from there they sailed to Cyprus.*

Note the partnership here: the Father, the Holy Spirit, and the church all were involved. The leadership of the church sent out these two men, but it was God's plan for their lives, and it took the ministry of the Holy Spirit to communicate and confirm the assignment.
In his farewell instructions to the elders of the church in Ephesus, Paul reminded them that it was the Holy Spirit who had made them overseers, and that they needed to be faithful in pastoring God's church:

Acts 20:28
*Therefore take heed to yourselves and to all the flock, among which the **Holy Spirit has made you overseers**, to shepherd the church of God which He purchased with His own blood.*

The Holy Spirit also played a role when Timothy was set in place as a church leader. His calling was confirmed by prophecy, which is one of the gifts of the Spirit:

1 Timothy 4:14
*Do not neglect the gift that is in you, which was given to you **by prophecy** with the laying on of the hands of the eldership.*

God the Father does the selecting and appointing of individuals for specific callings and assignments (Romans 8:28-30; 11:29; 1 Corinthians 1:1). However, it takes the ministry of the Holy Spirit to reveal God's will and enable us to carry it out.

(17) The Holy Spirit transforms us.

One of the most unique aspects of Christianity is the dynamic way that the Lord changes our lives. He alone is able to redeem and transform us into His likeness:

2 Corinthians 3:18
*But we all, with unveiled face, beholding as in a mirror the glory of the Lord, are being **transformed** into the same image from glory to glory, just as **by the Spirit of the Lord**.*

Romans 12:2
*And do not be conformed to this world, but be **transformed** by the renewing of your mind, that you*

may prove what is that good and acceptable and perfect will of God.

(18) The Holy Spirit sanctifies us.

Sanctification is the process by which believers are made holy (set apart, pure). Although we are saved by grace through faith in Jesus Christ and receive His righteousness at salvation, the Holy Spirit perfects us and conforms us to the character of Christ through sanctification:

1 Corinthians 6:11
And such were some of you. But you were washed, but you were ***sanctified****, but you were justified in the name of the Lord Jesus and* ***by the Spirit of our God****.*

2 Thessalonians 2:13
But we are bound to give thanks to God always for you, brethren beloved by the Lord, because God from the beginning chose you for salvation through ***sanctification by the Spirit*** *and belief in the truth.*

The Word and the blood of Jesus are also essential in this process:

Ephesians 5:25-26
25 *Husbands, love your wives, just as Christ also loved the church and gave Himself for her,*
26 *that He might sanctify and cleanse her with the washing of water* ***by the word****.*

Hebrews 13:12
Therefore Jesus also, that He might sanctify the people ***with His own blood****, suffered outside the gate.*

(19) The Holy Spirit produces godly fruit in us.

The development of the "fruit of the Spirit" is of major importance in the Holy Scriptures. It takes the work of the Holy Spirit to produce this fruit in the life of believers:

> Galatians 5:22-23 (NIV)
> 22 *But* ***the fruit of the Spirit*** *is love, joy, peace, patience, kindness, goodness, faithfulness,*
> 23 *gentleness and self-control. Against such things there is no law.*

In this passage, the Apostle Paul is referring to the work of the Holy Spirit in our lives. It is the Spirit who produces in us the very character traits that are found in the nature of Jesus. These traits are produced as we abide (live and remain) in Him. Jesus taught this in John 15:

> John 15:4-5
> 4 ***"Abide*** *in Me, and I in you. As the branch cannot bear fruit of itself, unless it* ***abides*** *in the vine, neither can you, unless you* ***abide*** *in Me.*
> *5 I am the vine, you are the branches. He who* ***abides*** *in Me, and I in him, bears much fruit..."*

Many people try to be good and do the right things, but here Jesus points out that the way to bear good fruit is by staying connected to Him. Godly character is not developed simply through human effort, but by relying and drawing on the Holy Spirit's power.

The meaning of the word "fruit" in these passages is not limited to godly virtues alone. It speaks of what a Christian **is** (character) and what he **does** (behavior). It also implies productivity. With the power of His Spirit, we are to exemplify the love of Jesus, causing others to know Him more and advancing His kingdom on earth:

John 15:16-17 (NIV)
16 *"You did not choose me, but I chose you and appointed you to go and* ***bear fruit****—fruit that will last. Then the Father will give you whatever you ask in my name.*
17 *This is my command: Love each other."*

As we maintain a right relationship with Jesus, the Holy Spirit enables us to be fruitful, and this glorifies the Father:

John 15:8
"By this My Father is glorified, that you bear much fruit; so you will be My disciples."

(20) The Holy Spirit empowers us to do the work of the Lord.

We have seen how the Holy Spirit enables believers to be Christlike by His work **in** us. Furthermore, He calls us to not only have the love of Christ, but to put this love into action (1 John 3:18). The Holy Spirit works **through** us to bless others. He empowers us for ministry.

Jesus told His disciples that the Holy Spirit would come and give them power. He said this in the context of the Great Commission, meaning that they would need supernatural power to preach the Gospel to the nations:

Luke 24:46-49 (NIV)
46 *He told them, "This is what is written: The Christ will suffer and rise from the dead on the third day,*
47 *and repentance and forgiveness of sins will be preached in his name to all nations, beginning at Jerusalem.*

48 *You are witnesses of these things.*
49 *I am going to send you what my Father has promised; but stay in the city until you have been clothed with* ***power from on high****."*

Acts 1:8
"But you shall receive ***power*** *when the Holy Spirit has come upon you; and you shall be witnesses to Me in Jerusalem, and in all Judea and Samaria, and to the end of the earth."*

Ephesians 3:20
Now to Him who is able to do exceedingly abundantly above all that we ask or think, according to the ***power*** *that works in us...*

Through the power of the Holy Spirit we are able to do great things. He prepares and anoints us for ministry:

1 John 2:20
But you have an anointing from the Holy One, and you know all things.

1 John 2:27
But the anointing which you have received from Him abides in you...

It was the Holy Spirit who anointed and empowered Jesus to accomplish His earthly ministry:

Luke 4:18-19
18 *"The Spirit of the LORD is upon Me, Because He has anointed Me To preach the gospel to the poor; He has sent Me to heal the brokenhearted, To proclaim liberty to the captives And recovery of sight to the blind, To set at liberty those who are oppressed;*
19 *To proclaim the acceptable year of the LORD."*

Acts 10:38
...God anointed Jesus of Nazareth with the Holy Spirit and with power, who went about doing good and healing all who were oppressed by the devil, for God was with Him.

Jesus performed astounding miracles through the power of the Holy Spirit. And to enable us to continue the work of Jesus, the Holy Spirit ministers His supernatural gifts through us. These are called the "gifts of the Spirit":

1 Corinthians 12:7-11
7 *But* ***the manifestation of the Spirit*** *is given to each one for the profit of all:*
8 *for to one is given the word of wisdom through the Spirit, to another the word of knowledge through the same Spirit,*
9 *to another faith by the same Spirit, to another gifts of healings by the same Spirit,*
10 *to another the working of miracles, to another prophecy, to another discerning of spirits, to another different kinds of tongues, to another the interpretation of tongues.*
11 *But one and the same Spirit works all these things, distributing to each one individually as He wills.*

It is important to point out that these are the gifts **of the Spirit**. Since these are His gifts (not ours), it is He who distributes these spiritual gifts as He wills. In other words, He decides who exercises which gift, how, and when.

The unique thing about this is the way in which the believer participates. There is a cooperation between the Holy Spirit and us. He works with us and through us.

Another important truth concerning the gifts of the Spirit is that an individual does not have to be perfect in order to be used by the Holy Spirit. In 1 Corinthians 12, where Paul discusses the gifts, he repeatedly uses forms of the Greek word *charismata,* which means "gifts of grace." The person ministered to receives the particular gift by grace, and the one ministering the gift does so by grace.

However, there is a balance between the gifts of the Spirit and the fruit of the Spirit. There is no doubt that the Lord is concerned about our **walk** and not just our **work**. In fact, we are to "walk in the Spirit" (Galatians 5:16, 25). As we do so, we will overcome the works of the flesh, and the love of God will motivate our actions. Operating in the gifts without the fruit of love produces very little. Paul emphasized this in his letter to the church at Corinth:

> 1 Corinthians 13:1-3
> 1 *Though I speak with the tongues of men and of angels, but have not love, I have become sounding brass or a clanging cymbal.*
> 2 *And though I have the gift of prophecy, and understand all mysteries and all knowledge, and though I have all faith, so that I could remove mountains, but have not love, I am nothing.*
> 3 *And though I bestow all my goods to feed the poor, and though I give my body to be burned, but have not love, it profits me nothing.*

Great faith, spiritual gifts, acts of charity, personal sacrifice, and miracle-working power are to be motivated by love.

But some take this important truth to an extreme and conclude, "I don't need the gifts. I'd rather have just the fruit." No, we need both the fruit and the gifts.

There is an important parallel in the epistle of James:

> James 2:14-18
> 14 *What does it profit, my brethren, if someone says he has faith but does not have works? Can faith save him?*
> 15 *If a brother or sister is naked and destitute of daily food,*
> 16 *and one of you says to them, "Depart in peace, be warmed and filled," but you do not give them the things which are needed for the body, what does it profit?*
> 17 *Thus also faith by itself, if it does not have works, is dead.*
> 18 *But someone will say, "You have faith, and I have works." Show me your faith without your works, and I will show you my faith by my works.*

Love, like faith, requires action. Just as faith is expressed by works, love is expressed by action. This is what the Apostle John said in his letter:

> 1 John 3:18 (TLB)
> *Little children, let us stop just* ***saying*** *we love people; let us* ***really*** *love them, and* ***show it*** *by our* ***actions****.*

Jesus is our prime example. Jesus, who was full of love, demonstrated that love by ministering to the needs of the people. When the crowd was hungry, He did not just say, "I love you," and send them away, but He performed a miracle and fed the multitude. Over and over again we read that He was moved with compassion and healed the sick, freed the oppressed, and raised the dead. Having the fruit alone would not have accomplished all these things. Power was also needed. Since He had both the fruit and the power, mighty signs, wonders, and miracles took place, and multitudes experienced the kingdom of God.

Both the fruit of the Spirit and the gifts of the Spirit are essential for effective ministry. In order to meet people's needs, both are vital. Trying to minister with one but not the other will result in imbalance.

We have considered some of the functions of the precious Holy Spirit and how He was at work throughout the Old and New Testaments. The continual presence of the Holy Spirit in our lives as modern New Testament believers is the basis for all the other benefits we have enumerated.

Another significant New Testament blessing began on the day of Pentecost in Acts 2 when the risen Lord Jesus poured out God's Spirit upon believers, filling them with additional power. This outpouring is called the baptism in the Holy Spirit. It is also called "the Pentecostal experience," "the infilling of the Holy Spirit," or "the charismatic renewal."

The baptism in the Holy Spirit has many facets, but its primary purpose is empowering believers to witness and to bring people into God's kingdom. This is perhaps why the devil has brought in so much confusion and division over this topic. In this book we will focus on the power of the Holy Spirit in the lives of Christians. We need more of this power to be Christlike and to carry out His ministry.

THREE TYPES OF BAPTISMS

For the sake of clarity, it is important to point out that the Bible speaks of more than one baptism.

In the book of Hebrews, the six foundational Christian doctrines are enumerated—repentance, faith, baptisms, laying on of hands, the resurrection, and eternal judgment:

> Hebrews 6:1-2
> 1 *Therefore, leaving the discussion of the elementary principles of Christ, let us go on to perfection, not laying again the foundation of repentance from dead works and of faith toward God,*
> 2 *of the doctrine of baptisms, of laying on of hands, of resurrection of the dead, and of eternal judgment.*

In the first part of verse 2, speaking of "the doctrine of baptisms," the Greek manuscripts use a plural form of the noun *baptisma,* which means baptism, dipping, washing, or the process of immersion or submersion.

The Greek verb is *baptizo*, which means to baptize, to dip, to immerse, or to submerge. Originally this verb did not have a religious meaning. This word was used in the business of dyeing fabrics, as well as for washing. The use of this word in the context of dyeing and washing clearly meant that something was being dipped, immersed, or submerged into a liquid. For example, a form of the verb *baptizo* is used when speaking about washing oneself, such as one's hands, which means that the hands are immersed into water (Mark 7:4; Luke 11:38). When a cloth is dipped into a dye, it changes color. Similarly, when we are baptized into Christ we take on His likeness.

In this chapter, we will briefly discuss the three baptisms that relate to our topic.

(1) The Baptism of John

The baptism of John was preached and practiced by John the Baptist, who was a forerunner of Jesus. It was a baptism of repentance. John admonished people to repent of their sins and to be baptized in water as a symbol of cleansing and purification. This was to prepare the people for their coming Messiah and His kingdom:

> Mark 1:4-5
> 4 *John came baptizing in the wilderness and preaching a baptism of repentance for the remission of sins.*
> 5 *Then all the land of Judea, and those from Jerusalem, went out to him and were all baptized by him in the Jordan River, confessing their sins.*

Crowds of people came to be baptized by John the Baptist in the Jordan River, repenting and confessing their sins. John challenged the self-righteous to change and to bear good fruit:

> Matthew 3:5-10
> 5 *Then Jerusalem, all Judea, and all the region around the Jordan went out to him*
> 6 *and were baptized by him in the Jordan, confessing their sins.*
> 7 *But when he saw many of the Pharisees and Sadducees coming to his baptism, he said to them, "Brood of vipers! Who warned you to flee from the wrath to come?*
> 8 *Therefore bear fruits worthy of repentance,*

> 9 *and do not think to say to yourselves, 'We have Abraham as our father.' For I say to you that God is able to raise up children to Abraham from these stones.*
> 10 *And even now the ax is laid to the root of the trees. Therefore every tree which does not bear good fruit is cut down and thrown into the fire."*

Since the purpose of John's baptism was to prepare people spiritually for the coming of Jesus, this baptism was later replaced by Christian baptism.

(2) Christian Baptism (Water Baptism)

Another important baptism that we see in Scripture is Christian baptism. This baptism is a sacrament (a holy ritual) formalizing an individual's conversion to Christ. It is a meaningful ceremony established by Jesus Himself:

> Matthew 28:18-20
> 18 *And Jesus came and spoke to them, saying, "All authority has been given to Me in heaven and on earth.*
> 19 *Go therefore and make disciples of all the nations,* ***baptizing*** *them in the name of the Father and of the Son and of the Holy Spirit,*
> 20 *teaching them to observe all things that I have commanded you; and lo, I am with you always, even to the end of the age." Amen.*

> Mark 16:15-16
> 15 *And He said to them, "Go into all the world and preach the gospel to every creature.*
> 16 *He who believes and is* ***baptized*** *will be saved; but he who does not believe will be condemned."*

Christian baptism is similar to John's baptism in two ways: both involve water, and both follow repentance and confession of sin. The Apostle Peter made this very clear on the day of Pentecost, when the people asked what they were to do in order to be saved:

> Acts 2:37-38
> 37 *Now when they heard this, they were cut to the heart, and said to Peter and the rest of the apostles, "Men and brethren, what shall we do?"*
> 38 *Then Peter said to them, "**Repent**, and let every one of you be baptized in the name of Jesus Christ for the remission of sins; and you shall receive the gift of the Holy Spirit."*

Peter's instructions to the people were to repent and be baptized. Repentance is the first step to salvation. But another key element of Christian baptism is faith. Jesus emphasized this by saying that one must believe:

> Mark 16:16
> *"He who **believes** and is baptized will be saved; but he who does not believe will be condemned."*

So Christian baptism not only involves repentance and the confession of sins, but also placing one's faith in Jesus Christ. It is through faith in Jesus and His atoning death and resurrection that an individual is saved and justified:

> John 1:12-13
> 12 *But as many as received Him, to them He gave the right to become children of God, to those who **believe** in His name:*
> 13 *who were born, not of blood, nor of the will of the flesh, nor of the will of man, but of God.*

John 3:16-18
16 *"For God so loved the world that He gave His only begotten Son, that whoever* ***believes*** *in Him should not perish but have everlasting life.*
17 *For God did not send His Son into the world to condemn the world, but that the world through Him might be saved.*
18 *He who* ***believes*** *in Him is not condemned; but he who does not believe is condemned already, because he has not believed in the name of the only begotten Son of God."*

The emphasis in Christian baptism is on believing in Jesus. It is not the sacrament of water baptism itself that saves an individual, but rather faith in Jesus Christ. The outward act of being baptized is a public acknowledgment that through faith in Jesus, an inward change has already taken place in that individual. At that time, the individual is baptized in the name of Jesus or "baptized into Christ," as the Bible puts it:

Galatians 3:26-27
26 *For you are all sons of God through faith in Christ Jesus.*
27 *For as many of you as were* ***baptized into Christ*** *have put on Christ.*

The phrase "baptized into Christ" denotes that an individual puts his faith and trust in Jesus Christ, and that he identifies with His death and resurrection:

Romans 6:3-5
3 *Or do you not know that as many of us as were baptized into Christ Jesus were baptized into His death?*
4 *Therefore we were buried with Him through baptism into death, that just as Christ was raised*

from the dead by the glory of the Father, even so we also should walk in newness of life.
5 *For if we have been united together in the likeness of His death, certainly we also shall be in the likeness of His resurrection.*

This passage gives the spiritual significance of water baptism. Just as Jesus died, was buried, and rose from the dead, the believer is symbolically "buried" in the baptismal water. The "old man," meaning his old sinful nature, is left behind, dead and buried. When the believer comes up out of the water, he is a "new man," resurrected to new life with Jesus. Not only are his past sins washed away, but the power of sin is broken, and he can now enjoy new life, free from bondage to sin.

Because they both include water and repentance, the baptism of John and Christian baptism may be mistaken by some to be the same thing. However, these two baptisms are distinct. John's baptism was for that time period, in order to prepare for Christ's coming. That is why some who had been baptized only into John's baptism were later re-baptized in the name of Jesus. This is what happened at Ephesus when the Apostle Paul witnessed to some of John's disciples and led them to the Lord (Acts 19:1-7). We will look at that event later.

(3) The Baptism in the Holy Spirit

The third baptism that we will examine is the baptism in the Holy Spirit. This is a spiritual experience in which the risen Lord Jesus imparts the Holy Spirit to believers, empowering them for ministry.

There are several Scriptures that use the verb *baptizo* in connection with the Holy Spirit. John the Baptist said that he baptized with water, but that Jesus would baptize with the Holy Spirit. All four Gospel writers considered his declaration important enough to record:

> Matthew 3:11
> *"I indeed baptize you with water unto repentance, but He who is coming after me is mightier than I, whose sandals I am not worthy to carry. He will baptize you with the Holy Spirit and fire."*

> Mark 1:8
> *"I indeed baptized you with water, but He will baptize you with the Holy Spirit."*

> Luke 3:16
> *John answered, saying to all, "I indeed baptize you with water; but One mightier than I is coming, whose sandal strap I am not worthy to loose. He will baptize you with the Holy Spirit and fire."*

> John 1:33
> *"I did not know Him, but He who sent me to baptize with water said to me, 'Upon whom you see the Spirit descending, and remaining on Him, this is He who baptizes with the Holy Spirit.'"*

The baptism in the Holy Spirit was not only prophesied by John (and others), but the risen Lord Jesus Himself told His disciples that they would be baptized in the Spirit:

> Acts 1:5
> *"for John truly baptized with water, but you shall be baptized with the Holy Spirit not many days from now."*

The first instance of the baptism in the Holy Spirit took place ten days after Jesus said this to His disciples. He had spoken with them and told them many things to prepare them for the coming of the Holy Spirit (John 14:16-18; 15:26; 16:7-14). Then before He left to go to heaven, Jesus commanded them to wait in Jerusalem for the coming of the Holy Spirit (Luke 24:49; Acts 1:4). After waiting in the Upper Room for ten days, the disciples and many others—120 people in all—were baptized in the Holy Spirit. Chapters 1 and 2 of the book of Acts record some of the events that took place during those days. In Acts 2 we read about the actual outpouring:

> Acts 2:1-4
> 1 *When the Day of Pentecost had fully come, they were all with one accord in one place.*
> 2 *And suddenly there came a sound from heaven, as of a rushing mighty wind, and it filled the whole house where they were sitting.*
> 3 *Then there appeared to them divided tongues, as of fire, and one sat upon each of them.*
> 4 *And they were all filled with the Holy Spirit and began to speak with other tongues, as the Spirit gave them utterance.*

This outpouring of the Holy Spirit on the day of Pentecost was indeed the "baptism in the Holy Spirit" that John the Baptist and Jesus had foretold. The Apostle Peter, who was filled with the Holy Spirit on the day of Pentecost, later used the word "baptized" to describe the experience:

> Acts 11:15-16
> 15 *"And as I began to speak, the Holy Spirit fell upon them, as upon us at the beginning.*
> 16 *Then I remembered the word of the Lord, how He said, 'John indeed baptized with water, but you shall be baptized with the Holy Spirit.'"*

Although some Bible translations use the preposition "with" when they write about Holy Spirit baptism, a more frequent translation of the Greek preposition *en* is "in." A believer is baptized **in** water and he is baptized **in** the Holy Spirit. With water baptism the person typically goes down into the water, but with Spirit baptism the Holy Spirit is poured out from heaven upon the individual. As this outpouring takes place, the person being baptized is immersed in the Spirit.

The Prophet Joel had foretold that the Spirit would be poured out:

> Joel 2:28
> *"And it shall come to pass afterward*
> *That I will* ***pour out*** *My Spirit on all flesh...."*

Peter declared the same thing on the day of Pentecost:

> Acts 2:17
> *"And it shall come to pass in the last days, says God,*
> *That I will* ***pour out*** *of My Spirit on all flesh..."*

> Acts 2:33
> *"Therefore being exalted to the right hand of God, and having received from the Father the promise of the Holy Spirit, He* ***poured out*** *this which you now see and hear."*

Other Scriptures confirm that the Holy Spirit falls or comes down upon individuals:

> Acts 2:2-4
> 2 *And suddenly there came a sound from heaven, as of a rushing mighty wind, and it filled the whole house where they were sitting.*

> 3 *Then there appeared to them divided tongues, as of fire, and one* ***sat upon*** *each of them.*
> 4 *And they were all filled with the Holy Spirit and began to speak with other tongues, as the Spirit gave them utterance.*

> Acts 10:44
> *While Peter was still speaking these words, the Holy Spirit* ***fell upon*** *all those who heard the word.*

> Acts 11:15
> *"And as I began to speak, the Holy Spirit* ***fell upon*** *them, as upon us at the beginning."*

> Acts 19:6
> *And when Paul had laid hands on them, the Holy Spirit* ***came upon*** *them, and they spoke with tongues and prophesied.*

Whether the Holy Spirit was poured upon, sat upon, fell upon, or came upon individuals, the picture portrayed is that of the Holy Spirit coming down from heaven upon the believers.

Another verb phrase that is often used in the New Testament concerning the work of the Holy Spirit is "to fill with." He wants to fill us with Himself:

> Acts 2:4
> *And they were all* ***filled with*** *the Holy Spirit...*

> Acts 9:17
> *..."Brother Saul, the Lord Jesus, who appeared to you on the road as you came, has sent me that you may receive your sight and be* ***filled with*** *the Holy Spirit."*

These Bible verses are the basis for the use of the term "the infilling of the Holy Spirit." The phrase "filled with the Spirit" is certainly descriptive of the effect that the baptism in the Holy Spirit has on the believer.

The actions discussed above express what the Holy Spirit does. There is also action required on the part of believers. They must **receive**:

> John 7:37-38
> 37 *On the last day, that great day of the feast, Jesus stood and cried out, saying, "If anyone thirsts, let him come to Me and* ***drink****.*
> 38 *He who believes in Me, as the Scripture has said, out of his heart will flow rivers of living water."*

> John 20:22
> *And when He had said this, He breathed on them, and said to them, "****Receive*** *the Holy Spirit."*

> Acts 10:47
> *"Can anyone forbid water, that these should not be baptized who have* ***received*** *the Holy Spirit just as we have?"*

Jesus spoke in metaphors about "drinking" spiritually and about the Holy Spirit flowing like "rivers of living water." Just as an individual drinks water and is filled, he receives the infilling of God's Spirit by faith. Once the believer is filled with the Spirit, the anointing can flow out to others like "rivers of living water."

The Bible has a lot more to say about the baptism in the Holy Spirit, and we will examine some of these truths in the next chapters.

THE BAPTISM IN THE HOLY SPIRIT IS DISTINCT FROM SALVATION

One very important and basic truth that must be established is that the baptism in the Holy Spirit is a distinct experience from salvation and water baptism. When we receive Jesus, we receive His Spirit in us, but we do not receive all of His **power** at that time. One can be a Christian with God's Spirit living in him and yet not be baptized in the Holy Spirit.

This might be compared to having a houseguest. When someone comes into your home, all of that person is present, but you do not have all of his possessions. In the same way, at salvation, we have all of the Holy Spirit in our lives—He is a whole Person—but we do not have all of His power.

A careful examination of the experiences of the original disciples and the early church reveals that Spirit baptism is in addition to salvation and water baptism.

Two Spiritual Experiences of the Disciples

Let us examine two major spiritual experiences that took place in the lives of the disciples.

(1) Salvation

One major supernatural experience in the lives of the original disciples took place on the evening of Resurrection Sunday. Shortly after the Lord Jesus rose from the dead, He appeared to His disciples. This event is recorded in John 20:

> John 20:19-23
> 19 *Then, the same day at evening, being the first day of the week, when the doors were shut where the disciples were assembled, for fear of the Jews, Jesus came and stood in the midst, and said to them, "Peace be with you."*
> 20 *When He had said this, He showed them His hands and His side. Then the disciples were glad when they saw the Lord.*
> 21 *So Jesus said to them again, "Peace to you! As the Father has sent Me, I also send you."*
> 22 *And when He had said this,* ***He breathed on them****, and said to them, "***Receive the Holy Spirit***.*
> 23 *If you forgive the sins of any, they are forgiven them; if you retain the sins of any, they are retained."*

This was a significant event in the spiritual life of those disciples. John 20:22 records that Jesus breathed on them and said to them, "Receive the Holy Spirit." We believe that this is when the disciples were saved.

There are at least three schools of thought concerning **when** the disciples were saved. Some Christians believe that this must have happened at some point while they were being discipled by Jesus. Others point to this passage in John 20 as the moment they were born again. Still others think that the disciples were saved at Pentecost. We do not wish to be dogmatic or take issue with anyone who disagrees with us on this question, because nowhere does Scripture say, "At this moment the disciples were saved." It is our perspective that the disciples were saved when the resurrected Jesus breathed His Spirit into them as recorded in John 20:22. Here is the reason we have reached this conclusion: first of all, it would be difficult to maintain that the disciples had already been saved before Jesus rose from the dead, because belief in the resurrection of Jesus is a requirement for salvation. This is clearly stated by the Apostle Paul in Romans 10:

> Romans 10:9 (NIV)
> *...if you confess with your mouth, "Jesus is Lord," and believe in your heart that God raised him from the dead, you will be saved.*

This Scripture gives two requirements for salvation. The disciples had already met the first requirement by putting their faith in Him (John 2:11; Matthew 16:16-20), but they had not met the second requirement, since Jesus had not yet died and risen from the dead. The atonement for their sins was not made until His crucifixion and resurrection. When Jesus appeared to the disciples that evening, He purposely showed them the wounds in His hands and His side as evidence of His resurrection (John 20:20). He was alive! They now believed that God had raised Him from death, and this fulfilled the second requirement for their salvation, that is, belief in the resurrection of Jesus. Any individual who confesses that Jesus is Lord and believes that God has raised Him from the dead is a Christian, and the Holy Spirit then lives in him.

Jesus had revealed this truth to His disciples earlier:

> John 14:16-17
> 16 *"And I will pray the Father, and He will give you another Helper, that He may abide with you forever—*
> 17 *the Spirit of truth, whom the world cannot receive, because it neither sees Him nor knows Him; but you know Him for* ***He dwells with you and will be in you.*** *"*

Jesus had told the disciples, "But you know Him, for He dwells **with** you and will be **in** you." This implies different levels of relationship with the Holy Spirit. Jesus was saying that the disciples knew the Holy Spirit and that He was involved in their lives, but they would later experience more of the Spirit, and He would be **in** them.

We have shown in the first chapter that the Holy Spirit comes to indwell the believer at the time of salvation. We saw in John 20:22 that Jesus said, "Receive the Holy Spirit," when He breathed on them on Resurrection Sunday. Therefore, we believe that this encounter fulfilled the John 14 passage—the Holy Spirit came into them at that time, and they were saved.

It is also significant that on Resurrection Sunday Jesus breathed on the disciples (John 20:22). With His breath, He imparted God's life-giving Spirit. The Greek word for spirit, *pneuma,* can also be translated "breath" or "wind."

Just as God the Father had breathed into Adam's nostrils and he came alive physically (Genesis 2:7), Jesus the Son now breathed on the disciples and they came alive spiritually. At that moment they were "saved" or "born again." The Holy Spirit came to live in them from that time on. Jesus had emphasized the importance of the new birth to Nicodemus:

> John 3:3-8
> 3 *Jesus answered and said to him, "Most assuredly, I say to you, unless one is* ***born again****, he cannot see the kingdom of God."*
> 4 *Nicodemus said to Him, "How can a man be born when he is old? Can he enter a second time into his mother's womb and be born?"*
> 5 *Jesus answered, "Most assuredly, I say to you,*

unless one is born of water and the Spirit, he cannot enter the kingdom of God.
6 *That which is born of the flesh is flesh, and that which is born of the Spirit is spirit.*
7 *Do not marvel that I said to you, '**You must be born again**.'*
8 *The wind blows where it wishes, and you hear the sound of it, but cannot tell where it comes from and where it goes. So is everyone who is born of the Spirit."*

We do not believe the disciples experienced salvation on the day of Pentecost. First of all, as we have seen, before Pentecost they had already confessed Jesus as Lord, and they believed in his resurrection.

Second, after Jesus went to heaven but before Pentecost, at the meeting when Judas was replaced, those present were identified as "believers" (literally "brothers"):

Acts 1:15 (NIV)
*In those days Peter stood up among the **believers** (a group numbering about a hundred and twenty)...*

Third, the purpose of salvation is receiving Jesus as Savior, but the purpose of the baptism in the Holy Spirit is empowering the believer—two separate experiences.

In conclusion, the disciples were saved. They were believers in the risen Lord Jesus. Their salvation was a major supernatural event. But although Jesus breathed on them and imparted the Holy Spirit to them, they still needed something more. If they had received the baptism in the Holy Spirit at the moment they were saved, then Jesus would not have commanded them to wait in Jerusalem to receive power from on high (Luke 24:49). They needed an additional experience.

(2) The Baptism in the Holy Spirit

Another major experience in the life of the original disciples was the baptism in the Holy Spirit.

As we have seen, Jesus had given His disciples new life in the Spirit and they were born again, but they had not yet been baptized in the Holy Spirit.

The normal biblical pattern is that salvation precedes the infilling of the Holy Spirit. Before we can receive the baptism in the Spirit, we must believe in Jesus. When He spoke about the Spirit's coming, He revealed this truth:

> John 7:37-39 (NASB)
> 37 *Now on the last day, the great day of the feast, Jesus stood and cried out, saying, "If anyone is thirsty, let him come to Me and drink.*
> 38 *He* ***who believes in Me****, as the Scripture said, 'From his innermost being will flow* ***rivers of living water****.'"*
> 39 *But this He spoke of the* ***Spirit****, whom those* ***who believed in Him*** *were to receive; for the Spirit was not yet given, because Jesus was not yet glorified.*

The two phrases, "he who believes in Me" and "those who believed in Him," clearly describe people who were already believers. The phrase, "rivers of living water," represents the Holy Spirit. This is explained by John in verse 39. Jesus was announcing the giving of the Spirit, an event that would take place later, after His ascension.

Before Jesus ascended into heaven, He commanded His disciples to wait in Jerusalem to receive "the Promise of the Father" before going out to minister. Jesus knew that in order for them to undertake the Great Commission to take the Gospel to the nations, they needed the power of the Holy Spirit:

> Luke 24:49 (NASB)
> *"And behold, I am sending forth the promise of My Father upon you; but you are to stay in the city until you are clothed with power from on high."*
>
> Acts 1:4-5
> 4 *And being assembled together with them, He commanded them not to depart from Jerusalem, but to wait for the Promise of the Father, "which," He said, "you have heard from Me;*
> 5 *for John truly baptized with water, but you shall be baptized with the Holy Spirit not many days from now."*

In obedience to Jesus' command, the original disciples were among the 120 believers who waited in the Upper Room in Jerusalem:

> Acts 1:12-15
> 12 *Then they returned to Jerusalem from the mount called Olivet, which is near Jerusalem, a Sabbath day's journey.*
> 13 *And when they had entered, they went up into the upper room where they were staying: Peter, James, John, and Andrew; Philip and Thomas; Bartholomew and Matthew; James the son of Alphaeus and Simon the Zealot; and Judas the son of James.*
> 14 *These all continued with one accord in prayer and supplication, with the women and Mary the mother of Jesus, and with His brothers.*
> 15 *And in those days Peter stood up in the midst of the disciples (altogether the number of names was about a hundred and twenty)...*

Ten days later, on Pentecost, the Spirit came upon them:

> Acts 2:1-4 (NIV)
> 1 *When the day of Pentecost came, they were all together in one place.*
> 2 *Suddenly a sound like the blowing of a violent wind came from heaven and filled the whole house where they were sitting.*
> 3 *They saw what seemed to be tongues of fire that separated and came to rest on each of them.*
> 4 *All of them were filled with the Holy Spirit and began to speak in other tongues as the Spirit enabled them.*

These were believers. They had already experienced salvation, and they had the Holy Spirit living in them. But now they received the power Jesus had told them about:

> Acts 1:8
> *"But you shall receive* ***power*** *when the Holy Spirit has come upon you; and you shall be witnesses to Me in Jerusalem, and in all Judea and Samaria, and to the end of the earth."*

The emphasis here is on power. The Greek word used here for power, *dunamis*, means miraculous strength, ability, or "dynamite" power. The disciples received it when they were baptized in the Holy Spirit. This mighty power enables believers to impact the world with the Gospel.

In examining the experiences of the original disciples, we have seen that salvation and the baptism in the Holy Spirit are distinct. In salvation, the emphasis is on receiving Jesus as our Savior, but in the baptism in the Holy Spirit, the emphasis is on receiving supernatural power. The disciples were born again by the Spirit (John 20:22, 3:6), and they were later baptized in the Holy Spirit (Acts 2:4).

The Baptism in the Spirit after Pentecost

The outpouring of the Holy Spirit on Pentecost was not the only recorded instance of the Spirit being poured out. Later in the book of Acts, we find other accounts of the Spirit coming upon individuals after Pentecost. These events also show that salvation and the baptism in the Holy Spirit are distinct. It is important for our study to examine some of these post-Pentecostal experiences.

(1) The Believers in Samaria (Acts 8)

In Acts 8 we read that Philip, one of the men chosen to help the apostles in Acts 6, went to Samaria to preach the Gospel. The Samaritans saw that the power and authority of Jesus rested on Philip, and they listened to him. They believed in Jesus and were baptized with water.

When the apostles at Jerusalem heard what had happened in Samaria, they sent Peter and John. When they arrived, they prayed for these new believers to receive the baptism in the Holy Spirit:

> Acts 8:5-17
> 5 *Then Philip went down to the city of Samaria and preached Christ to them.*
> 6 *And the multitudes with one accord heeded the things spoken by Philip, hearing and seeing the miracles which he did.*
> 7 *For unclean spirits, crying with a loud voice, came out of many who were possessed; and many who were paralyzed and lame were healed.*
> 8 *And there was great joy in that city.*
> 9 *But there was a certain man called Simon, who previously practiced sorcery in the city and*

> *astonished the people of Samaria, claiming that he was someone great,*
> 10 *to whom they all gave heed, from the least to the greatest, saying, "This man is the great power of God."*
> 11 *And they heeded him because he had astonished them with his sorceries for a long time.*
> 12 *But when* ***they believed*** *Philip as he preached the things concerning the kingdom of God and the name of Jesus Christ, both men and women* ***were baptized****.*
> 13 *Then Simon himself also believed; and when he was baptized he continued with Philip, and was amazed, seeing the miracles and signs which were done.*
> 14 *Now when the apostles who were at Jerusalem heard that Samaria had received the word of God, they sent Peter and John to them,*
> 15 *who, when they had come down, prayed for them that they might receive the Holy Spirit.*
> 16 *For as yet He had fallen upon none of them. They* ***had only been baptized in the name of the Lord Jesus****.*
> 17 *Then they laid hands on them, and* ***they received the Holy Spirit****.*

This Scripture clearly records that the Samaritans' receiving the Holy Spirit was a separate experience from their receiving salvation. They were saved by hearing and receiving the Word of God through the preaching of Philip the evangelist. The Bible says that they accepted his message, believed, and were baptized in the name of the Lord Jesus. So at that time these individuals were saved.

If the baptism in the Holy Spirit takes place simultaneously with salvation—as some suppose—then why would the apostles in Jerusalem have needed to send Peter and John to pray for these believers to receive the

Holy Spirit? Verse 16 makes it even more clear, when it states that the Holy Spirit had fallen upon none of them up to that time. These Samaritans had been saved through the ministry of Philip, but they had not yet received the baptism in the Holy Spirit. They were baptized in the Holy Spirit through the ministry of Peter and John when they laid hands on them. This is the first time that the laying on of hands to help impart the Holy Spirit is recorded.

(2) The Gentiles in Caesarea (Acts 10)

Another outpouring of the Spirit took place at Caesarea, which was a center of the Roman occupational forces. Here a God-fearing Roman officer named Cornelius was told by an angel to send for Peter, who was staying in the city of Joppa.

Up to this point the apostles thought that salvation and the baptism in the Holy Spirit were for the Jews only. So Peter was hesitant to go tell Gentiles about Jesus and the baptism in the Holy Spirit. If a Gentile (non-Jew) wanted to receive Jesus, he was expected to first become a Jew and come under all the requirements of Jewish law.

However, the Lord made it clear to Peter, through a vision and by direct instructions, that he was to go with the men who had come to get him. To his amazement, when he got to Cornelius' house and began to tell the Gentiles there about Jesus, the Spirit fell on all who heard the Word:

> Acts 10:44-48 (NASB)
> 44 *While Peter was still speaking these words,* ***the Holy Spirit fell upon*** *all those who were listening to the message.*

> 45 *All the circumcised believers who came with Peter were amazed, because the gift of* ***the Holy Spirit had been poured out on*** *the Gentiles also.*
> 46 *For they were hearing them speaking with tongues and exalting God. Then Peter answered,*
> 47 *"Surely no one can refuse the water for these to be baptized* ***who have received the Holy Spirit*** *just as we did, can he?"*
> 48 *And he ordered them to be baptized in the name of Jesus Christ. Then they asked him to stay on for a few days.*

What happened at Cornelius' house is somewhat different from what happened in Acts 2 and in Acts 8. In this instance they were first baptized in the Holy Spirit and then baptized in water. However, when one considers these events, one realizes that here again the baptism in the Holy Spirit is a distinct experience from salvation and water baptism.

At Cornelius' house, the Holy Spirit fell upon the people gathered there as they were listening to Peter share about Jesus. They were all baptized in the Holy Spirit and spoke in other tongues.

While Peter was preaching, they received the message, believed in Jesus, and were saved. After putting their faith in Jesus, they were baptized in the Holy Spirit and spoke in other tongues. Hearing them speak in tongues was a convincing sign that they had indeed been baptized in the Holy Spirit. No one could doubt or negate this experience. In fact, Peter related this to the experience he had had on the day of Pentecost by saying, "…who have received the Holy Spirit just as we did…" (verse 47).

When Peter returned to Jerusalem, the Jewish believers contended with him for associating with Gentiles. He told them what had happened at Cornelius' house:

> Acts 11:15-18 (NASB)
> 15 *"And as I began to speak,* ***the Holy Spirit fell upon them just as He did upon us at the beginning****.*
> 16 *And I remembered the word of the Lord, how He used to say, 'John baptized with water, but you will be baptized with the Holy Spirit.'*
> 17 *Therefore if God gave to them the same gift as He gave to us also* ***after believing in the Lord Jesus Christ****, who was I that I could stand in God's way?"*
> 18 *When they heard this, they quieted down and glorified God, saying, "Well then, God has granted to the Gentiles also the repentance that leads to life."*

Here again Peter is emphasizing that these Gentiles had experienced salvation and the baptism in the Holy Spirit, just as the original disciples had years before. Verse 17 confirms that believing in Jesus normally comes first, and then receiving the Gift of the Holy Spirit with the evidence of speaking in tongues.

So the Jewish believers realized that the Gospel was for Gentiles also. Salvation and the baptism in the Holy Spirit are separate experiences and are available to all.

(3) The Twelve Men at Ephesus (Acts 19)

Some twenty years after the first outpouring in chapter two of Acts, Paul made a third trip to Ephesus, and there he found twelve of John the Baptist's disciples. He asked them if they had received the Holy Spirit, but they said they had only been baptized into John's baptism.

As we have seen, John's baptism was a baptism of repentance, stressing man's sinfulness and need for forgiveness. When Paul found out that these men had only experienced John's baptism, he led them to accept Jesus and baptized them with water in the name of Jesus. Then he laid his hands upon them to receive the Holy Spirit. The Holy Spirit came upon them, and they spoke in tongues and prophesied:

> Acts 19:1-7
> 1 *And it happened, while Apollos was at Corinth, that Paul, having passed through the upper regions, came to Ephesus. And finding some disciples*
> 2 *he said to them, "**Did you receive the Holy Spirit when you believed**?" So they said to him, "We have not so much as heard whether there is a Holy Spirit."*
> 3 *And he said to them, "Into what then were you baptized?" So they said, "Into John's baptism."*
> 4 *Then Paul said, "John indeed baptized with a baptism of repentance, saying to the people that they should believe on Him who would come after him, that is, on Christ Jesus."*
> 5 *When they heard this, **they were baptized** in the name of the Lord Jesus.*
> 6 *And when Paul had laid hands on them, **the Holy Spirit came upon them**, and they spoke with tongues and prophesied.*
> 7 *Now the men were about twelve in all.*

The very fact that Paul asked these men if they had received the Holy Spirit when they believed confirms that the baptism in the Holy Spirit does not happen automatically. If the two experiences were the same, or automatic, then such a question would have been unnecessary. Paul asked the question because he knew that it is indeed possible for someone to be saved, but not be baptized in the Holy Spirit.

The sequence of events that followed also confirms this point. Once Paul found out that these were John's disciples, he told them about Jesus, they believed in Him, and they were re-baptized in the name of the Lord Jesus (verse 5).

Some people would think that Paul's leading them to the Lord and water-baptizing them in the name of Jesus would be all that they would need. But we see that Paul did not stop with salvation and water baptism, but he proceeded to lay his hands on them, and when he did, they were baptized in the Holy Spirit. We know that they received the Holy Spirit, because immediately they began to speak in other tongues and prophesy (verse 6). Paul did not have to ask them again if they had received, or if anything special had happened to them when he prayed for them. He knew they had been filled with the Holy Spirit because he heard them speaking in tongues. Even though these experiences happened consecutively, they were distinct.

What happened with these men is also a good example of how, when one receives the Holy Spirit (the Gift), he can be used by the Spirit to minister any of His gifts as He wills (1 Corinthians 12:7-11). They received the Spirit and immediately the prophetic anointing came upon them.

Besides the events we have discussed, there are other Scriptures that reveal that other believers received the baptism in the Holy Spirit. From Paul's letter to the Corinthians, we know that the believers at Corinth were baptized in the Holy Spirit and spoke in tongues and prophesied (1 Corinthians 14). And of course Paul himself was filled with the Holy Spirit and spoke in tongues (Acts 9:17; 1 Corinthians 14:18).

The various Holy Spirit outpourings recorded in the Bible share some common characteristics. First, the baptism in the Holy Spirit is distinct from salvation. Second, the baptism in the Spirit is for believers. In addition, this experience may happen in various ways, but speaking in tongues is almost always involved. This is the most frequent manifestation or sign that confirms that an individual has been baptized in the Holy Spirit.

If salvation and the baptism in the Holy Spirit were the same experience, then the original disciples would have spoken in tongues on Resurrection Sunday when Jesus breathed on them, and the people in Samaria would not have needed Peter and John to come pray for them in order to be filled with the Spirit. In Samaria, just as in Ephesus and Caesarea, the infilling of the Spirit was a separate event. The people at these various places received an infilling similar to the one the original disciples had experienced. These outpourings took place over a period of two decades. Biblical evidence has clearly shown that the baptism in the Holy Spirit is distinct from salvation. These experiences are still happening today.

THE BAPTISM IN THE HOLY SPIRIT IS AN EXPERIENCE FOR TODAY

The work and the gifts of the Holy Spirit, including speaking in tongues, did not cease with the end of the early church, but have impacted the lives of Christians for the past two thousand years. God promised that in the last days He would pour out His Spirit on all.

After the Holy Spirit was poured out on the day of Pentecost, the Apostle Peter told the crowd gathered there that what they had just witnessed was what the Prophet Joel had foretold (Joel 2:28-29):

> Acts 2:14-18 (NIV)
> 14 *Then Peter stood up with the Eleven, raised his voice and addressed the crowd: "Fellow Jews and all of you who live in Jerusalem, let me explain this to you; listen carefully to what I say.*
> 15 *These men are not drunk, as you suppose. It's only nine in the morning!*
> 16 *No, this is what was spoken by the prophet Joel:*
> 17 *'In the* ***last days****, God says, I will pour out my Spirit on* ***all people****. Your sons and daughters will prophesy, your young men will see visions, your old men will dream dreams.*
> 18 *Even on my servants, both men and women, I will pour out my Spirit in those days, and they will prophesy.'"*

Then when the people asked Peter and the other apostles what they were to do, he answered them without hesitation:

Acts 2:38-39 (NIV)
38 *Peter replied, "Repent and be baptized, every one of you, in the name of Jesus Christ for the forgiveness of your sins. And you will receive the gift of the Holy Spirit.*
39 *The promise is for you and your children and for all who are far off—for all whom the Lord our God will call."*

Both Joel and Peter declared that the outpouring of the Spirit is for **all** people from all walks of life—including men and women, sons and daughters, young and old—and considering what happened in Acts 10, we can add Jews and Gentiles.

Furthermore, in verse 39 Peter told the believers that "the Promise is for you and your children and for all who are far off..." The "Promise" refers to the baptism in the Holy Spirit. Although the Holy Spirit comes to indwell the believer at the time of salvation, this use of the word "Promise" correlates with Jesus' telling the disciples to wait in Jerusalem to be filled with the power of the Holy Spirit, a separate experience from their salvation:

Luke 24:49
"Behold, I send ***the Promise of My Father*** *upon you; but tarry in the city of Jerusalem until you are endued with power from on high."*

Acts 1:4-5
4 *And being assembled together with them, He commanded them not to depart from Jerusalem, but to wait for* ***the Promise of the Father****, "which," He said, "you have heard from Me;*
5 *for John truly baptized with water, but you shall be baptized with the Holy Spirit not many days from now."*

Interpreting Acts 2:39 in light of these passages makes it clear that the baptism in the Holy Spirit was not just for the early believers, but for all Christians, present, past, and future. The phrases "in the last days" (Acts 2:17) and "for all who are far off" (Acts 2:39) confirm that the outpouring of the Spirit did not come to an end. If the disciples lived in the last days, how much more do we live in the last days!

Hebrews 13:8 tells us that Jesus Christ is the same yesterday, today, and forever. He still saves, and He still baptizes in the Holy Spirit. He has not changed, and we are still in the era of the Holy Spirit that began on the day of Pentecost. Jesus promised that the Holy Spirit would be with us forever (John 14:16). He is still with us, and we still need Him.

The call to witness is just as great today as it was in the early church. God loves everyone in all generations and wants everyone to be saved (John 3:16; 1 Timothy 2:3-4). We need the fruit and the gifts of the Holy Spirit in order to evangelize the world. God would not expect us to do the work of bringing in the harvest of souls without giving us the power and the tools to do so. Jesus emphasized this by commanding the disciples to wait for the Holy Spirit (Luke 24:49). It is not God's nature to provide a gift with such an important purpose for only a period of time and then take it away.

We and many Christians in various churches and denominations today have experienced the authentic presence and power of the Holy Spirit. The Bible confirms that the baptism in the Holy Spirit is for every child of God and that this experience is for today.

JESUS IS THE BAPTIZER IN THE HOLY SPIRIT

John the Baptist announced Jesus as both the Savior and the Baptizer in the Holy Spirit:

> John 1:29-36
> 29 *The next day John saw Jesus coming toward him, and said, "Behold! The Lamb of God who takes away the sin of the world!*
> 30 *This is He of whom I said, 'After me comes a Man who is preferred before me, for He was before me.'*
> 31 *I did not know Him; but that He should be revealed to Israel, therefore I came baptizing with water."*
> 32 *And John bore witness, saying, "I saw the Spirit descending from heaven like a dove, and He remained upon Him.*
> 33 *I did not know Him, but He who sent me to baptize with water said to me, 'Upon whom you see the Spirit descending, and remaining on Him, this is He who baptizes with the Holy Spirit.'*
> 34 *And I have seen and testified that this is the Son of God."*
> 35 *Again, the next day, John stood with two of his disciples.*
> 36 *And looking at Jesus as He walked, he said, "Behold the Lamb of God!"*

In his declarations, John the Baptist identified two unique ministries that Jesus would have. In verses 29 and 36, he proclaimed Jesus to be the Savior of the world, and in verse 33, he declared Him to be the Baptizer in the Holy Spirit. This is also recorded in Matthew 3:11, Mark 1:8, and Luke 3:16.

John had been told by the Father that the One upon whom he saw the Spirit descend and remain would be the One who would baptize with the Holy Spirit. The fulfillment of this visible sign (verse 32) confirmed that Jesus was the Baptizer in the Holy Spirit. Jesus did not baptize people with water, although His disciples did (John 4:1-2). Perhaps the reason He refrained from doing this was to make it clear that He had a different baptism to do.

Not only did John the Baptist testify that Jesus is the Baptizer in the Holy Spirit, but Jesus also declared Himself to be the Giver of the Holy Spirit:

> John 15:26
> *"But when the Helper comes, whom* ***I shall send*** *to you from the Father, the Spirit of truth who proceeds from the Father, He will testify of Me."*

> John 16:7
> *"Nevertheless I tell you the truth. It is to your advantage that I go away; for if I do not go away, the Helper will not come to you; but if I depart,* ***I will send*** *Him to you."*

> Luke 24:49
> *"Behold,* ***I send*** *the Promise of My Father upon you; but tarry in the city of Jerusalem until you are endued with power from on high."*

By proclaiming Jesus as the Baptizer in the Holy Spirit, John was in essence prophesying the outpouring of the Spirit. Jesus referred to the Holy Spirit as "the Promise of the Father" (Acts 1:4) and promised to send Him.

When the Spirit was poured out, the prophecy and the promise were fulfilled. Peter confirmed this and then stated that it was indeed Jesus who had poured out the Holy Spirit:

> Acts 2:33
> *Therefore being exalted to the right hand of God, and having received from the Father the promise of the Holy Spirit,* ***He poured*** *out this which you now see and hear.*

Jesus is well able to impart the Holy Spirit to anyone without our help, but the Lord often uses Spirit-filled Christians to minister to others. In previous sections we have shared biblical examples of this (Acts 8:14-17, Acts 9:17, Acts 19:6). We have also witnessed it first hand. Ever since He filled us with His Spirit in 1975, we have seen others used to help people receive the baptism in the Holy Spirit, and this has been a vital part of our calling as well.

Like salvation, Spirit baptism is a powerful, life-changing experience, but we need to continually keep in mind whose power this is. We must remind ourselves and others that the power comes from God. Although we teach and encourage other Christians, and even pray for them to experience Spirit baptism, we do not baptize them in the Holy Spirit. Jesus does. When Ananias laid hands on Paul (Acts 9:17), he knew that he was not the Baptizer. When Peter reported the Spirit baptism of the Gentiles at Cornelius' house, he made it very clear that it was the Lord who had given them the Gift (Acts 11:17). And when Paul laid hands on the believers in Ephesus (Acts 19), he knew that he was not the Baptizer. Jesus is.

Hebrews 13:8 says that Jesus is the same yesterday, today, and forever. This means that Jesus still saves, and He still baptizes people in the Holy Spirit.

WHEN WAS THE HOLY SPIRIT FIRST POURED OUT?

On the Day of Pentecost

It is clear from Scripture that the Holy Spirit was first poured out on the day of Pentecost, fifty days after Jesus' resurrection, ten days after His ascension into heaven.

There were seven feasts instituted by God in the Old Testament. All male Jews were required to observe the three major feasts: the Feast of Passover, the Feast of Pentecost, and the Feast of Tabernacles. Each of these was sacred for the Israelites, and each has a special meaning for Christians. The feasts of the Old Covenant foreshadow events of the New Covenant. When God instituted these feasts, He established the specific times when they were to be observed. The significance and timing of these feasts should not be overlooked.

Passover was the first feast of the year (Exodus 12:1-50; Numbers 28:16-25; Deuteronomy 16:1-8). This feast originated the night when the Angel of Death **passed over** the houses of the Israelites who had placed the blood of a perfect lamb on their doorposts at the time of the exodus from Egypt. Each Passover, the Jews commemorated God's delivering them from slavery and death. The applying of the blood to the doorposts foreshadowed the salvation of anyone who would appropriate the blood of Jesus, the Lamb of God, who came to take away the sin of the world (John 1:29). The prophetic fulfillment occurred almost 1500 years later at the exact time of the Feast of Passover, when Jesus died on the cross as our perfect sacrifice.

Fifty days after Passover, or seven weeks counting from the day after the Sabbath of the Passover, was the Feast of Pentecost (Leviticus 23:15-21; Deuteronomy 16:9-12). The word "Pentecost" comes from the Greek word *pentekostē*, meaning "fiftieth," with the word "day" understood. In the Old Testament it is called "the Feast of Weeks," or "the Feast of Harvest." This feast was observed during the summer harvest. The Jews were to celebrate God's goodness by presenting the first fruits of their new grain crop as an offering to the Lord. The fulfillment of the Feast of Pentecost took place precisely fifty days after Jesus' resurrection, when He poured out the Holy Spirit from heaven upon the 120 believers. Through that empowerment, Peter preached the Gospel on Pentecost and about 3,000 people were saved (Acts 2:41). Those new converts were the beginning of the great spiritual harvest through the power of the Holy Spirit.

The Feast of Pentecost also commemorated God's giving of the law at Mount Sinai. There are some meaningful parallels between the event at Mount Sinai and the Pentecostal experience in Acts 2. At both times there were visible signs of the presence or the glory of God. At Mount Sinai, the Lord came down upon the mountain with thunder and lightning, and His glory was like a consuming fire (Exodus 19:16-18; 24:17). On the day of Pentecost, there came a sound from heaven like a rushing mighty wind, and there were divided tongues like flames that came to rest upon each of the 120 believers (Acts 2:2-3). With the giving of the law at Mount Sinai, God was establishing a holy nation. With the outpouring of the Holy Spirit at the Feast of Pentecost, Jesus was establishing a holy church. Pentecost ushered in a new era—the covenant of grace. The law came by Moses, but grace and truth came through Jesus (John 1:17). The law is no longer written on tablets of stone, but on new hearts given by His Spirit (Ezekiel 36:26-28).

Many Christians now look forward to the day when Jesus will return and fulfill the third major feast, the Feast of Tabernacles, which is also known as "the Feast of Ingathering" (Numbers 29:12-39; Deuteronomy 16:13). This festival was to be observed after Passover and after Pentecost, after all the remaining crops had been gathered in the fall. During this festival, the Jews lived in booths (tabernacles) to commemorate their journey through the wilderness to the Promised Land. In addition, they offered sacrifices of thanksgiving for the ingathering of the produce. The fulfillment of this feast will take place at the appointed time, when the trumpet of God will sound, and Jesus will return in glory to gather all believers and dwell with them forever (1 Thessalonians 4:16). Before this can happen, His Spirit-empowered witnesses must take the Gospel to all nations (Matthew 24:14).

During the feasts, the Children of Israel remembered their past and renewed their trust in God. These were times of commemorating and celebrating His provision and protection. As we consider these festivals from a New Testament perspective, we see God's great love for us in His redeeming us from the bondage of sin (Passover), His empowering us to bring others to Him (Pentecost), and His returning for us to spend eternity with Him (Tabernacles).

We have seen that by God's divine plan, the Holy Spirit was poured out during the Feast of Harvest, which is most commonly known as Pentecost. But one may still ask, "Why did this have to take place at that particular Pentecost? Why wasn't the Spirit poured out earlier?"

After Jesus Was Glorified

The outpouring of the Holy Spirit had to be done at the right time. Jesus could not send the Holy Spirit until He had completed His mission (John 3:16-17; Luke 4:18-19) and until He had been glorified. The direct connection between Jesus' being glorified and the giving of the Holy Spirit is noted in the Gospel of John:

> John 7:37-39
> 37 *On the last day, that great day of the feast, Jesus stood and cried out, saying, "If anyone thirsts, let him come to Me and drink.*
> 38 *He who believes in Me, as the Scripture has said, out of his heart will flow rivers of living water."*
> 39 *But this He spoke concerning the Spirit, whom those believing in Him would receive; for* ***the Holy Spirit was not yet given, because Jesus was not yet glorified****.*

What does it mean that "Jesus was not yet glorified"? It means that Jesus had to die, be raised from the dead, and be exalted to the right hand of the Father before the outpouring of the Spirit could take place. The Apostle Paul connects the promise of the Spirit to the redemptive work of Jesus on the cross:

> Galatians 3:13-14
> 13 *Christ has redeemed us from the curse of the law, having become a curse for us (for it is written, "Cursed is everyone who hangs on a tree"),*
> 14 *that the blessing of Abraham might come upon the Gentiles in Christ Jesus, that we might receive the promise of the Spirit through faith.*

According to this passage, the way we receive the Holy Spirit is through faith in Jesus.

As the sacrificial Lamb of God, Jesus died on the cross in our place. His mission was not finalized until He entered the heavenly Holy of Holies and presented Himself before God. As our Great High Priest, He had to present His blood before the Father in order to complete the atonement. So He was both the High Priest and the Sacrifice. This is explained in Hebrews 9:

> Hebrews 9:11-15, 22-28 (NIV)
> 11 *When Christ came as high priest of the good things that are already here, he went through the greater and more perfect tabernacle that is not man-made, that is to say, not a part of this creation.*
> 12 *He did not enter by means of the blood of goats and calves; but he entered the Most Holy Place once for all by his own blood, having obtained eternal redemption.*
> 13 *The blood of goats and bulls and the ashes of a heifer sprinkled on those who are ceremonially unclean sanctify them so that they are outwardly clean.*
> 14 *How much more, then, will the blood of Christ, who through the eternal Spirit offered himself unblemished to God, cleanse our consciences from acts that lead to death, so that we may serve the living God!*
> 15 *For this reason Christ is the mediator of a new covenant, that those who are called may receive the promised eternal inheritance—now that he has died as a ransom to set them free from the sins committed under the first covenant.*
> 22 *In fact, the law requires that nearly everything be cleansed with blood, and without the shedding of blood there is no forgiveness.*
> 23 *It was necessary, then, for the copies of the heavenly things to be purified with these sacrifices, but the heavenly things themselves with better*

sacrifices than these.
24 *For Christ did not enter a man-made sanctuary that was only a copy of the true one; he entered heaven itself, now to appear for us in God's presence.*
25 *Nor did he enter heaven to offer himself again and again, the way the high priest enters the Most Holy Place every year with blood that is not his own.*
26 *Then Christ would have had to suffer many times since the creation of the world. But now he has appeared once for all at the end of the ages to do away with sin by the sacrifice of himself.*
27 *Just as man is destined to die once, and after that to face judgment,*
28 *so Christ was sacrificed once to take away the sins of many people...*

Jesus had to complete the sacrifice in order to provide not only our salvation, but also the Gift of the Holy Spirit. It is on the merits of Jesus, and not our own, that we receive from God. Once Jesus had finalized our atonement, He could impart the promised Holy Spirit to believers.

The Apostle Peter confirmed this in his sermon to the crowd after the Spirit had been gloriously poured out on the day of Pentecost:

Acts 2:32-33
32 *This Jesus God has raised up, of which we are all witnesses.*
33 *Therefore being exalted to the right hand of God, and having received from the Father the promise of the Holy Spirit, He poured out this which you now see and hear.*

When Peter said that Jesus had been "raised up" and "exalted," this was a significant declaration, confirming that the Lord had been glorified.

Jesus had told His followers in advance about His leaving and promised that He would send the Holy Spirit to them:

> John 16:7
> *"Nevertheless I tell you the truth. It is to your advantage that I go away; for if I do not go away, the Helper will not come to you; but if I depart, I will send Him to you."*

Jesus' leaving the earth and going to heaven was essential for the coming of the Holy Spirit in a whole new way. After Jesus went to heaven, the Holy Spirit then became the main divine Representative on earth.

Of course, this does not mean that the Holy Spirit was not active on earth before Pentecost. He has been involved throughout history, all the way back to creation (Genesis 1:2). But, as we have said, the activity of the Holy Spirit was different in the Old Testament, typically involving particular individuals at particular times.

Jesus told His disciples that His going away would be to their advantage. One may wonder why that would be better. The benefit that the original disciples and all believers would have is that the Holy Spirit would be present in each of their lives at the same time. Even though the Holy Spirit is a Person in a very real sense, and not just a force or an influence, He is not limited by a physical body as Jesus was. Since He is a spiritual Person, He can be everywhere at the same time.

Another benefit associated with the coming of the Holy Spirit is that His presence is continuous. Jesus had previously assured His disciples of this:

John 14:16
*"And I will pray the Father, and He will give you another Helper, that He may abide with you **forever**."*

The Holy Spirit does not just come on special occasions to empower, inspire, or reveal something to someone, as He did in the Old Testament. Now He comes and indwells the believer and remains with him. We can enjoy His fellowship continuously.

In summary, the outpouring of the Holy Spirit took place at just the right time. There were certain events that had to take place in the proper order. The Holy Spirit could not come until Jesus had been glorified. And Jesus could not be glorified until He had completed His mission. Having fulfilled every requirement, Jesus was exalted and qualified to impart the Holy Spirit to those who believe.

In addition, when Jesus made atonement for sin on the cross, He also made anyone who believes in Him worthy and eligible to receive the precious Gift of the Holy Spirit.

THE PURPOSE AND IMPACT OF THE BAPTISM IN THE HOLY SPIRIT

Some may wonder what is the purpose of the baptism in the Holy Spirit. If one is already a believer and the Spirit is in him, why does he need the baptism in the Holy Spirit?

As we have already stated, the main purpose of the baptism in the Holy Spirit is to empower the believer. Jesus made this very clear to His disciples:

> Luke 24:49
> *"Behold, I send the Promise of My Father upon you; but tarry in the city of Jerusalem until you are endued with* ***power*** *from on high."*

> Acts 1:4-8
> 4 *And being assembled together with them, He commanded them not to depart from Jerusalem, but to wait for the Promise of the Father, "which," He said, "you have heard from Me;*
> 5 *for John truly baptized with water, but you shall be baptized with the Holy Spirit not many days from now."*
> 6 *Therefore, when they had come together, they asked Him, saying, "Lord, will You at this time restore the kingdom to Israel?"*
> 7 *And He said to them, "It is not for you to know times or seasons which the Father has put in His own authority.*
> 8 *But you shall receive* ***power*** *when the Holy Spirit has come upon you; and you shall be witnesses to Me in Jerusalem, and in all Judea and Samaria, and to the end of the earth."*

In this passage, Jesus speaks of the power that comes through the baptism in the Holy Spirit, and the main reason for having more power is in order to witness. The Pentecostal experience has many different aspects, but its primary purpose is empowering believers to witness and to bring unsaved people into God's kingdom.

Speaking of the baptism in the Holy Spirit to His disciples in Acts 1:8, Jesus gave answers as to **what** we receive, **when**, **why**, and **where**:

WHAT?	Power
WHEN?	When the Holy Spirit comes upon you
WHY?	To be His witnesses
WHERE?	In Jerusalem, Judea, Samaria, and to the end of the earth

The baptism in the Holy Spirit was of such importance that Jesus commanded His disciples to stay in Jerusalem until they had received "power from on high" before going out to minister (Luke 24:49; Acts 1:4-5). Each of them was to first be empowered by the Holy Spirit, and then go out from Jerusalem to evangelize the rest of the world.

In order for one to really appreciate the importance of the baptism in the Holy Spirit, one must consider the results or changes that this experience produced in the lives of the original disciples. In the next section we will look at their spiritual condition **before** Pentecost and **after**.

The Disciples before Pentecost

When we look specifically at the period between Jesus' arrest and Pentecost, we find that the disciples had little positive effect on people through their ministry. During that time, they did not have the power to significantly impact the world with their witness. Instead, the Bible records several incidents that indicate that these men were discouraged, fearful, and bewildered.

The evening that Jesus was arrested, His disciples deserted Him and fled:

> Matthew 26:56
> *...Then all the disciples forsook Him and fled.*

Peter had declared that he would lay down his life for the Lord (John 13:37-38), but while Jesus was on trial before the high priest, the scribes, and the elders, Peter denied three times that he knew Him:

> Matthew 26:69-75
> 69 *Now Peter sat outside in the courtyard. And a servant girl came to him, saying, "You also were with Jesus of Galilee."*
> 70 *But he denied it before them all, saying, "I do not know what you are saying."*
> 71 *And when he had gone out to the gateway, another girl saw him and said to those who were there, "This fellow also was with Jesus of Nazareth."*
> 72 *But again he denied with an oath, "I do not know the Man!"*
> 73 *And a little later those who stood by came up and said to Peter, "Surely you also are one of them, for your speech betrays you."*
> 74 *Then he began to curse and swear, saying, "I do not know the Man!" Immediately a rooster crowed.*

75 *And Peter remembered the word of Jesus who had said to him, "Before the rooster crows, you will deny Me three times." So he went out and wept bitterly.*

Peter's denial of the Lord was such a dramatic experience that all four Gospel writers record it. Even though he had strongly professed his commitment to Jesus, saying that he was ready to die for Him, he failed his challenge when confronted by people in the courtyard. Then Peter repented with bitter tears (verse 75). Later Jesus mercifully restored him to the ministry (John 21).

After Jesus had been taken from them, the disciples were afraid and hid behind closed doors:

John 20:19
Then, the same day at evening, being the first day of the week, when the doors were shut where the disciples were assembled, for fear of the Jews, Jesus came and stood in the midst, and said to them, "Peace be with you."

In addition, when the women came and told the disciples that Jesus had risen from the dead, they did not believe the women's report:

Luke 24:9-11
9 *Then they returned from the tomb and told all these things to the eleven and to all the rest.*
10 *It was Mary Magdalene, Joanna, Mary the mother of James, and the other women with them, who told these things to the apostles.*
11 *And their words seemed to them like idle tales, and they did not believe them.*

When Jesus appeared to the disciples on Resurrection Sunday, Thomas was not present. They told him that they had seen the Lord, but he did not believe their testimony:

> John 20:24-25
> 24 *Now Thomas, called the Twin, one of the twelve, was not with them when Jesus came.*
> 25 *The other disciples therefore said to him, "We have seen the Lord." So he said to them, "Unless I see in His hands the print of the nails, and put my finger into the print of the nails, and put my hand into His side, I will not believe."*

We are not trying to judge or criticize these men. It was natural for them to be upset and disheartened at what had happened to their Master. They had become dependent upon the physical presence of Jesus and had hopes that were now shattered.

But the point is that in spite of all they had learned from Jesus—what they had experienced, the miracles they had seen, and the ways He had prepared them for what was to come—in their own strength they were not able to maintain their faith and stand strong in time of adversity. Disappointment, discouragement, fear, doubt, and unbelief held them back. These were good men with good intentions, but they lacked the power to carry them out.

Then Jesus, after His resurrection and just before His ascension, commanded the disciples to wait in Jerusalem until they were filled with power from above. On the day of Pentecost, from His exalted place in heaven, Jesus poured out the Holy Spirit upon them. Now they had the Person and power of the Holy Spirit, and they were ready to impact the world with the Gospel.

The Disciples after Pentecost

The power of the Holy Spirit significantly changed the lives of the disciples.

(1) After Pentecost the disciples had power to pray.

The prayer life of the original disciples intensified after they were baptized in the Holy Spirit. They placed a high priority on prayer. For this reason, they set deacons in place to take care of other business so they could devote themselves to prayer and to teaching and preaching:

> Acts 6:4
> *but we will give ourselves continually to* ***prayer*** *and to the ministry of the word."*

Since prayer was so essential for the disciples, they took part in group prayer meetings, both in the temple and in homes. When Peter and John stopped and ministered healing to a lame man sitting at the Gate Beautiful, they were on their way to the afternoon prayer meeting at the temple:

> Acts 3:1 (TLB)
> *Peter and John went to the Temple one afternoon to take part in the three o'clock daily* ***prayer meeting****.*

After the healing of the crippled man, Peter and John were arrested by the Jewish leaders. The next day, they were released from custody and were commanded not to speak or preach in the name of Jesus. They immediately got together with other believers, and they had a powerful prayer meeting:

Acts 4:29-31
29 *Now, Lord, look on their threats, and grant to Your servants that with all boldness they may speak Your word,*
30 *by stretching out Your hand to heal, and that signs and wonders may be done through the name of Your holy Servant Jesus."*
31 *And when they had* ***prayed****, the place where they were assembled together was shaken; and they were all filled with the Holy Spirit, and they spoke the word of God with boldness.*

Prayer was not just vital to the apostles, but it was an essential component of the spiritual life of the early church. We see that the believers prayed often and fervently:

Acts 2:42
And they continued steadfastly in the apostles' doctrine and fellowship, in the breaking of bread, and in ***prayers****.*

Another scripture that reveals the empowered believers' prayer life is recorded in Acts 12. Herod Agrippa I put Peter in prison, and they prayed for him intensely:

Acts 12:5 (NIV)
So Peter was kept in prison, but the church was ***earnestly praying*** *to God for him.*

As a result of the believers' prayers, God sent an angel and set Peter free. Once released, he went immediately to the house of Mary, the mother of John Mark, where there was a prayer meeting going on:

Acts 12:12
So, when he had considered this, he came to the

> *house of Mary, the mother of John whose surname was Mark, where* ***many were gathered together praying****.*

Fervent prayers produce great results. Through the empowerment of the Holy Spirit, we can pray powerful prayers. A major benefit of the empowerment of the Holy Spirit is that He gives us the desire to pray and the ability to pray effectively.

(2) After Pentecost the disciples had power to preach.

After the outpouring of the Holy Spirit, the apostles proclaimed the Word with power. On that very day, the day of Pentecost, Peter spoke to the crowd with great boldness and 3,000 people were saved:

> Acts 2:40-41
> 40 *And with many other words he testified and exhorted them, saying, "Be saved from this perverse generation."*
> 41 *Then those who gladly received his word were baptized; and that day about three thousand souls were added to them.*

When the crippled man was healed, Peter addressed the people again and 5,000 men were saved:

> Acts 4:4
> *However, many of those who heard the word believed; and the number of the men came to be about five thousand..*

The apostles also preached with great boldness to the rulers and elders:

Acts 4:13
Now when they saw the ***boldness*** *of Peter and John, and perceived that they were uneducated and untrained men, they marveled. And they realized that they had been with Jesus.*

Acts 4:33
And with great ***power*** *the apostles gave witness to the resurrection of the Lord Jesus. And great grace was upon them all.*

The apostles were bold witnesses everywhere, even under persecution and hardship.

(3) After Pentecost the disciples had power to perform miracles.

Through the empowerment of the Spirit, the apostles walked in the miraculous. Their witness was not just in their words, but in the demonstration of the power of God (1 Corinthians 2:4-5). They ministered confidently in God's power and authority—so much so that many people brought their sick out into the streets, hoping that Peter's shadow would fall on them and heal them:

Acts 5:12-16
12 *And through the hands of the apostles many signs and wonders were done among the people. And they were all with one accord in Solomon's Porch.*
13 *Yet none of the rest dared join them, but the people esteemed them highly.*
14 *And believers were increasingly added to the Lord, multitudes of both men and women,*
15 *so that they brought the sick out into the streets and laid them on beds and couches, that at least the shadow of Peter passing by might fall on some of them.*

16 *Also a multitude gathered from the surrounding cities to Jerusalem, bringing sick people and those who were tormented by unclean spirits, and they were all healed.*

Acts 2:43 (NIV)
Everyone was filled with awe, and many wonders and miraculous signs were done by the apostles.

The apostles were not just preaching and teaching about Jesus. They were doing the same works that Jesus had done. He empowers every believer to do these works by the power of the Holy Spirit:

John 14:12
"Most assuredly, I say to you, he who believes in Me, the works that I do he will do also; and greater works than these he will do, because I go to My Father."

(4) After Pentecost the disciples had power to impact cities and regions.

Through the apostles' dynamic preaching and the profound miracles that were taking place, whole communities were affected.

First of all, the city of Jerusalem was greatly impacted. The healing of the lame man at the temple gate, followed by Peter's explanation of what had happened, resulted in the salvation of thousands in Jerusalem:

Acts 3:1-10
1 *Now Peter and John went up together to the temple at the hour of prayer, the ninth hour.*

> 2 *And a certain man lame from his mother's womb was carried, whom they laid daily at the gate of the temple which is called Beautiful, to ask alms from those who entered the temple;*
> 3 *who, seeing Peter and John about to go into the temple, asked for alms.*
> 4 *And fixing his eyes on him, with John, Peter said, "Look at us."*
> 5 *So he gave them his attention, expecting to receive something from them.*
> 6 *Then Peter said, "Silver and gold I do not have, but what I do have I give you: In the name of Jesus Christ of Nazareth, rise up and walk."*
> 7 *And he took him by the right hand and lifted him up, and immediately his feet and ankle bones received strength.*
> 8 *So he, leaping up, stood and walked and entered the temple with them—walking, leaping, and praising God.*
> 9 *And all the people saw him walking and praising God.*
> 10 *Then they knew that it was he who sat begging alms at the Beautiful Gate of the temple; and they were filled with wonder and amazement at what had happened to him.*

The people going in and out of the temple had seen this crippled man many times, sitting there begging for alms. Now when they saw him standing and walking, they knew that there was no other explanation but that the power of Jesus had healed him. Many were amazed at what had happened and believed in the Lord. Peter made it clear that it was faith in the name of Jesus that had made this man whole, and not the apostles' own power or godliness (Acts 3:11-16). The recently Spirit-baptized Peter spoke with authority and confidence to the crippled man and commanded him in the name of Jesus to arise and walk

(Acts 3:6). He did not petition God the Father for this man's healing, but rather as a representative of the Lord, he used the Name of Jesus and the power and authority inherent in that name.

The rulers and the elders themselves confirmed that the miracle was credible and known by all in Jerusalem:

> Acts 4:16
> *saying, "What shall we do to these men? For, indeed, that a notable miracle has been done through them is evident to all who dwell in Jerusalem, and we cannot deny it."*

As a result of the powerful ministry of the apostles, many were saved and the church grew:

> Acts 6:7
> *Then the word of God spread, and the number of the disciples multiplied greatly in Jerusalem, and a great many of the priests were obedient to the faith.*

From Jerusalem, the apostles traveled to other areas to evangelize. One of those places was the town of Lydda:

> Acts 9:32-35
> 32 *Now it came to pass, as Peter went through all parts of the country, that he also came down to the saints who dwelt in Lydda.*
> 33 *There he found a certain man named Aeneas, who had been bedridden eight years and was paralyzed.*
> 34 *And Peter said to him, "Aeneas, Jesus the Christ heals you. Arise and make your bed." Then he arose immediately.*
> 35 *So all who dwelt at Lydda and Sharon saw him and turned to the Lord.*

Peter spoke with authority and power, commanding the paralyzed man to arise. By his saying, "Aeneas, Jesus heals you" (verse 34), he made it clear that it was not Peter's power that would heal him, but the power of Jesus. As a result, those who saw the healing turned to the Lord. They were eyewitnesses of the power and authority of the resurrected Christ, and they gave their lives to Him. The whole region of Sharon was impacted by Peter's witness.

Another place influenced by the power of the Spirit working through the apostles was Joppa, the main seaport on the Mediterranean coast (modern Jaffa). In that city lived Dorcas, a Christian woman respected for her good deeds. After she became ill and died, she was raised from the dead by the power of the Holy Spirit through the ministry of Peter. As a result of that miracle of resurrection, many accepted Jesus:

> Acts 9:36-42
> 36 *At Joppa there was a certain disciple named Tabitha, which is translated Dorcas. This woman was full of good works and charitable deeds which she did.*
> 37 *But it happened in those days that she became sick and died. When they had washed her, they laid her in an upper room.*
> 38 *And since Lydda was near Joppa, and the disciples had heard that Peter was there, they sent two men to him, imploring him not to delay in coming to them.*
> 39 *Then Peter arose and went with them. When he had come, they brought him to the upper room. And all the widows stood by him weeping, showing the tunics and garments which Dorcas had made while she was with them.*

> 40 *But Peter put them all out, and knelt down and prayed. And turning to the body he said, "Tabitha, arise." And she opened her eyes, and when she saw Peter she sat up.*
> 41 *Then he gave her his hand and lifted her up; and when he had called the saints and widows, he presented her alive.*
> 42 *And it became known throughout all Joppa, and many believed on the Lord.*

This is clearly what we call "power evangelism." These apostles walked in such power and authority that everywhere they went, they brought change by the message they proclaimed and the miracles they performed in the name of Jesus. Jesus had told them that they would receive power when the Holy Spirit came upon them and that they would be His witnesses, beginning in Jerusalem and going out from there to other places. This is exactly what happened, and the results were phenomenal.

Our study has centered around the original disciples and the impact that the baptism in the Holy Spirit had upon their lives and ministry. However, we must not forget that there were many others who were also greatly affected by this experience and went out and ministered in the power of the Spirit—men like Philip, Ananias, Barnabas, Stephen, Paul, and others.

Stephen was full of faith and power. He operated in the miraculous and spoke with great wisdom. It was through the power of the Holy Spirit that he was able to maintain his faith and his witness, even while he was being stoned to death. In Acts 7:55 we read that he was full of the Holy Spirit, and that he looked up into heaven and saw the glory of God and Jesus standing at the Father's right hand.

In the midst of his agony, he knelt and prayed for those who were stoning him and yielded his spirit to the Lord (Acts 7:54-60).

Paul witnessed this event and later was miraculously saved and filled with the Holy Spirit (Acts 9). Through a supernatural encounter with God, he went from persecuting the church to preaching Christ and writing thirteen books of the New Testament. Much like the other apostles, he evangelized in the power of the Spirit, with signs and wonders following him.

This miraculous power is not just available to a few select individuals but to **every** believer. For the church today to impact the world with the Gospel of Jesus Christ, believers must walk in the same power as the apostles did in the book of Acts. Through their bold witness many were brought into the kingdom of God. Christianity spread and the church grew rapidly. The Lord of the Harvest is still looking for witnesses to go forth in the power of the Holy Spirit and bring in the harvest of souls. This is indeed the primary purpose of the baptism in the Holy Spirit.

The outward visible fruit produced through the lives of the apostles came as a result of the inward spiritual change that they had experienced. They overcame their natural fears, insecurities, and human weaknesses. This internal transformation came about through the power of the Holy Spirit. Although the baptism in the Holy Spirit is a one-time event, being filled with the Spirit is an ongoing process. In Acts 4:31 the apostles were again filled with the Holy Spirit, who enabled them to courageously overcome hardship, persecution, and temptation, and to be bold witnesses of the Gospel. In the same way, we are encouraged to continually be filled with the Holy Spirit (Ephesians 5:18).

If you desire to experience this kind of power in your personal walk with God, and to impact your world with the Gospel, the Lord has more for you, too.

SINS AGAINST THE HOLY SPIRIT

Since the Holy Spirit is a Person, He has a personality and feelings. As a Person, He speaks and performs tasks. In addition, He has a mind and a will (1 Corinthians 12:11; Romans 8:27).

The Holy Spirit is our constant Companion and He delights in our fellowship. How we respond to Him, whether in a positive or negative way, is crucial to our relationship. We can either honor and obey Him, or we can hinder His work. When we disregard or resist Him, not only do we miss out on His wonderful blessings, but we may also actually sin against Him.

The Holy Spirit and all of His gifts are not always embraced by Christians. Since one of the main purposes of the baptism in the Holy Spirit is to give us power to evangelize, the devil has tried to prevent this by bringing misunderstanding and division. Satan does not want the church to be powerful, and he may use many tactics to stop the spread of the Gospel. There is considerable doctrinal confusion about the scope and relevance of the Holy Spirit's ministry today. Many fear the unknown or the supernatural. In addition, some immature Christians may have misrepresented the Holy Spirit. We must overcome the distractions of the enemy and ascertain the truth in God's Word regarding the Holy Spirit. Believers must guard against using these or other excuses, which can cause us to sin against the Holy Spirit.

The Bible gives instructions about interacting with the Holy Spirit and specifically prohibits a number of sins against Him.

(1) Do not blaspheme against the Holy Spirit.

The most serious sin against the Holy Spirit is blasphemy. Jesus made this very clear:

> Mark 3:28-30 (NIV)
> 28 *"I tell you the truth, all the sins and **blasphemies** of men will be forgiven them.*
> 29 *But whoever **blasphemes against the Holy Spirit** will never be forgiven; he is guilty of an eternal sin."*
> 30 *He said this because they were saying, "He has an evil spirit."*

> Matthew 12:31-32 (NIV)
> 31 *"And so I tell you, every sin and blasphemy will be forgiven men, but the **blasphemy against the Spirit** will not be forgiven.*
> 32 *Anyone who speaks a word against the Son of Man will be forgiven, but anyone who speaks against the Holy Spirit will not be forgiven, either in this age or in the age to come."*

In general, the verb "to blaspheme" means to speak evil or irreverently, to curse, to defame, or to slander.

In the Old Testament, blaspheming God was a serious offense punishable by death (Leviticus 24:15-16).

Jesus was accused of blasphemy for claiming to be God's Son (Luke 5:21; Matthew 26:63-65).

However, the unpardonable sin is blasphemy against the Holy Spirit. Jesus said in Matthew 12:31 that every other kind of sin and blasphemy will be forgiven, but the blasphemy against the Spirit will not be forgiven.

As we look at this verse in its context, we see that the Pharisees were giving credit to Satan for the miracle that Jesus had performed in healing the demon-possessed man:

Matthew 12:22-32
22 *Then one was brought to Him who was demon-possessed, blind and mute; and* ***He healed him, so that the blind and mute man both spoke and saw****.*
23 *And all the multitudes were amazed and said, "Could this be the Son of David?"*
24 *Now when the Pharisees heard it they said, "This fellow does not cast out demons except by Beelzebub, the ruler of the demons."*
25 *But Jesus knew their thoughts, and said to them: "Every kingdom divided against itself is brought to desolation, and every city or house divided against itself will not stand.*
26 *If Satan casts out Satan, he is divided against himself. How then will his kingdom stand?*
27 *And if I cast out demons by Beelzebub, by whom do your sons cast them out? Therefore they shall be your judges.*
28 *But if I cast out demons by the Spirit of God, surely the kingdom of God has come upon you.*
29 *Or how can one enter a strong man's house and plunder his goods, unless he first binds the strong man? And then he will plunder his house.*
30 *He who is not with Me is against Me, and he who does not gather with Me scatters abroad.*
31 *Therefore I say to you, every sin and blasphemy will be forgiven men, but the blasphemy against the Spirit will not be forgiven men.*
32 *Anyone who speaks a word against the Son of Man, it will be forgiven him; but whoever speaks against the Holy Spirit, it will not be forgiven him, either in this age or in the age to come."*

The Pharisees accused Jesus of casting out demons by the power and authority of Beelzebub, the prince of demons. Beelzebub was the name of a Canaanite god that was adopted and worshiped by the Philistines. The Jews used that name to refer to Satan.

In giving Satan credit for the miracle Jesus had performed, the Pharisees were defaming and desecrating the Holy Spirit that had empowered Jesus to accomplish the miracle. Luke 4:18-19, Acts 10:38, and other Scriptures clearly state that Jesus was anointed with the Holy Spirit and His power, and that through that anointing He went everywhere doing good, healing, and setting the captives free. Such divine miracles are the work of the Holy Spirit (1 Corinthians 12).

Witnessing such a demonstration of divine power, and yet willfully and antagonistically declaring it to be Satanic, reveals a hopelessly hardened heart. This obstinate attitude of the Pharisees resulted in a deliberate rejection of the truth about Jesus and His ministry in the power of the Holy Spirit.

One of the reasons that blasphemy against the Holy Spirit is the most serious sin is because it takes the ministry of the Holy Spirit to convict us of sin, so that we can repent and come to Jesus. When we blaspheme against the Holy Spirit, we reject the very Person that can lead us to Jesus and enable us to walk in righteousness.

We must be careful that we do not refuse the message and ministry of the Holy Spirit. When He is at work, and His gifts and miracles are evident, we must not reject or speak against Him. Instead, we should submit to the Holy Spirit and be thankful for His presence and power among us.

(2) Do not insult the Holy Spirit.

Hebrews 10:26-29
26 *For if we sin willfully after we have received the knowledge of the truth, there no longer remains a sacrifice for sins,*
27 *but a certain fearful expectation of judgment, and fiery indignation which will devour the adversaries.*
28 *Anyone who has rejected Moses' law dies without mercy on the testimony of two or three witnesses.*
29 *Of how much worse punishment, do you suppose, will he be thought worthy who has trampled the Son of God underfoot, counted the blood of the covenant by which he was sanctified a common thing, and* ***insulted the Spirit of grace****?*

This passage was written to warn Jewish believers who were tempted to reject Jesus and return to Judaism. It also applies to anyone who willfully rejects Jesus after experiencing salvation and the work of the Holy Spirit. Since the Holy Spirit is the One who brings us to salvation, He is insulted when we deliberately reject Jesus and His sacrifice.

(3) Do not resist the Holy Spirit.

Stephen, one of the early deacons (Acts 6:5), was a man full of the Holy Spirit. He had great faith and wisdom, and he performed miracles by God's mighty power. Some opposed his ministry and gathered false witnesses against him. Forced to appear before the Sanhedrin, he responded:

Acts 7:51 (NIV)
"You stiff-necked people, with uncircumcised hearts and ears! You are just like your fathers: You always ***resist the Holy Spirit****!"*

The Jewish leaders were self-righteous and self-sufficient, trusting in their ritualism and traditions. They were circumcised physically, but not spiritually. Their consecration was outward and incomplete, so they were striving against the truth and resisting the work of the Holy Spirit.

We should be careful that by tradition, legalism, or ignorance we do not oppose or resist the work of the Holy Spirit. He delights in people who are hungry for the truth and fully submitted to His will.

(4) Do not rebel against the Holy Spirit.

During their time in the wilderness, the Israelites rebelled against the Holy Spirit, in spite of God's goodness and faithfulness to them:

> Isaiah 63:9-10
> 9 *In all their affliction He was afflicted, And the Angel of His Presence saved them; In His love and in His pity He redeemed them; And He bore them and carried them All the days of old.*
> 10 *But they **rebelled** and grieved His Holy Spirit; So He turned Himself against them as an enemy, And He fought against them.*

The verb "to rebel" means to oppose or contend against authority.

Rebelling against the Lord can bring serious consequences. In the above passage, God turned against them. Disobedience is very costly. The way to peace and victory is by yielding to and obeying the leading of the Holy Spirit and the Word of God.

(5) Do not grieve the Holy Spirit.

In his letter to the believers at Ephesus, the Apostle Paul gave some exhortations:

> Ephesians 4:29-32
> 29 *Let no corrupt word proceed out of your mouth, but what is good for necessary edification, that it may impart grace to the hearers.*
> 30 *And* ***do not grieve the Holy Spirit of God****, by whom you were sealed for the day of redemption.*
> 31 *Let all bitterness, wrath, anger, clamor, and evil speaking be put away from you, with all malice.*
> 32 *And be kind to one another, tenderhearted, forgiving one another, even as God in Christ forgave you.*

When we grieve someone, we cause pain, grief, or sorrow.

We grieve the Holy Spirit by the sins we commit. These may be things that we do, or things that we should do, but fail to do. The Holy Spirit can be grieved by our wrong thoughts, attitudes, words, motives, and actions. Some of these are identified in the passage above—harsh language, quarreling, anger, bitterness, and evil behavior.

Let's not cause the Holy Spirit sorrow by yielding to the desires of our sinful nature. Instead, let's please Him by demonstrating love, grace, and forgiveness. In our interpersonal relationships we should say and do only what will help and bless others.

(6) Do not quench the Holy Spirit.

Paul gave the Thessalonians several instructions and specifically told them not to quench the Holy Spirit:

1 Thessalonians 5:19
Do not quench the Spirit.

"To quench" means to put out (a fire), to extinguish, to suppress, or to stifle.

We can quench the Spirit in private or in a gathering when we ignore His leading or stifle His gifts. Right after saying not to quench the Spirit, Paul says, "Do not despise prophecies" (1 Thessalonians 5:20). And in 1 Corinthians 14:39, he says that speaking in tongues should not be forbidden.

Sometimes spiritual gifts are controversial and cause division. Instead of finding biblical answers, some Christians prefer to smother the gifts by discouraging their use. We should not stifle the work of the Holy Spirit, but rather encourage the operation of these gifts. The Bible tells us that we are to desire spiritual gifts, especially the gift of prophecy (1 Corinthians 14:1).

It is noteworthy that these commands were written to a church, not to unbelievers. Commanding the believers not to quench the Spirit implies that they were doing just that, or that it is possible for believers to do it. The flesh can get in the way of the Spirit.

Instead of hindering the move of the Spirit, believers should obey His promptings, in order to edify the church and advance God's kingdom.

(7) Do not lie to the Holy Spirit.

We read about the sin of lying to the Holy Spirit in Acts 5, when Ananias and Sapphira sold a piece of property and gave some of the money to the church, saying that they had given it all:

> Acts 5:1-5
> 1 *But a certain man named Ananias, with Sapphira his wife, sold a possession.*
> 2 *And he kept back part of the proceeds, his wife also being aware of it, and brought a certain part and laid it at the apostles' feet.*
> 3 *But Peter said, "Ananias, why has Satan filled your heart* ***to lie to the Holy Spirit*** *and keep back part of the price of the land for yourself?*
> 4 *While it remained, was it not your own? And after it was sold, was it not in your own control? Why have you conceived this thing in your heart? You have* ***not lied to men but to God****."*
> 5 *Then Ananias, hearing these words, fell down and breathed his last. So great fear came upon all those who heard these things.*

The sin was not that Ananias and Sapphira did not give all the income to the church. The sin was saying that they had given it all. They were dishonest. They had deliberately planned to lie about their offering.

Lying involves dishonesty, hypocrisy, and the intention to deceive. Satan is the great deceiver, and he is the father of lies (John 8:44).

Since the Holy Spirit is a Member of the Holy Trinity, lying to the Spirit is the same as lying to God (verse 4). God desires honesty. King David expressed this in his prayer of repentance:

> Psalm 51:6
> *Behold,* ***You desire truth*** *in the inward parts, And in the hidden part You will make me to know wisdom.*

Furthermore, the Holy Spirit is known as the Spirit of Truth (John 15:26). In order to walk in the Spirit we must walk in truth. When we walk in honesty and truthfulness, we please the Lord:

> Proverbs 12:22
> *Lying lips are an abomination to the LORD, But **those who deal truthfully are His delight**.*

This is not an all-inclusive study of the sins against the Holy Spirit. These Scriptures remind us that the Holy Spirit is a Person—God Himself—and that our wrong attitudes and actions hurt Him. In addition, if we hinder the Holy Spirit, we are hindering the Gift that Jesus sent to enable us to be effective ministers of the Gospel. For all He is and for all He does, we should esteem the Holy Spirit and desire more of His presence in our lives.

These truths are encapsulated in Paul's letter to the Ephesians:

> Ephesians 4:30 (The Message)
> *Don't grieve God. Don't break his heart. His Holy Spirit, moving and breathing in you, is the most intimate part of your life, making you fit for himself. Don't take such a gift for granted.*

COMMON QUESTIONS ABOUT THE BAPTISM IN THE HOLY SPIRIT

Here are some questions that we are often asked, and that you, or someone you know, may have concerning the baptism in the Holy Spirit.

(1) Is the baptism in the Holy Spirit for today? Who can receive it?

Yes, the baptism in the Holy Spirit is for today. It is for **all** believers, without regard to age, race, gender, or denomination. It is for everyone, every time, every place! It's for anyone who believes in Jesus and is thirsty for more of Him. Note His words in John 7:

> John 7:37-39
> 37 *On the last day, that great day of the feast, Jesus stood and cried out, saying, "If anyone thirsts, let him come to Me and drink.*
> 38 *He who believes in Me, as the Scripture has said, out of his heart will flow rivers of living water."*
> 39 *But this He spoke concerning the Spirit, whom those believing in Him would receive; for the Holy Spirit was not yet given, because Jesus was not yet glorified.*

Many years before, the Prophet Joel prophesied about the outpouring of the Holy Spirit and declared that it is for all (Joel 2:28-29).

On the day of Pentecost, Peter referred to Joel's prophecy when he addressed the crowd:

Acts 2:16-18
16 "*But this is what was spoken by the prophet Joel:*
17 *'And it shall come to pass in the last days, says God, That I will pour out of My Spirit on all flesh; Your sons and your daughters shall prophesy, Your young men shall see visions, Your old men shall dream dreams.*
18 *And on My menservants and on My maidservants I will pour out My Spirit in those days; And they shall prophesy.'"*

Acts 2:38-39 (NIV)
38 *Peter replied, "Repent and be baptized, every one of you, in the name of Jesus Christ for the forgiveness of your sins. And you will receive the gift of the Holy Spirit.*
39 *The promise is for you and your children and for all who are far off—for all whom the Lord our God will call."*

These Scriptures confirm that the baptism in the Holy Spirit is for all Christians today.

(2) Do I have to have the baptism in the Holy Spirit in order to go to heaven?

No, you do not have to have the baptism in the Holy Spirit in order to go to heaven. In order to be saved, you must repent of your sins, believe in Jesus, and confess Him as your Savior and Lord:

John 3:16
"For God so loved the world that He gave His only begotten Son, that whoever believes in Him should not perish but have everlasting life."

Acts 4:12 (NIV)
Salvation is found in no one else, for there is no other name under heaven given to men by which we must be saved.

Romans 10:9-10 (NIV)
9 *...if you confess with your mouth, "Jesus is Lord," and believe in your heart that God raised him from the dead, you will be saved.*
10 *For it is with your heart that you believe and are justified, and it is with your mouth that you confess and are saved.*

(3) Since the baptism in the Holy Spirit is not required for salvation, why do I need it?

The baptism in the Holy Spirit is a baptism of power. It empowers the believer in every area of life. Our relationship with God, our Bible study, our prayer life, and our witness are all strengthened. Jesus said that we would receive power when we receive the Holy Spirit:

Acts 1:8
"But you shall receive power when the Holy Spirit has come upon you; and you shall be witnesses to Me in Jerusalem, and in all Judea and Samaria, and to the end of the earth."

In addition, the fruit of the Spirit is more evident after receiving the baptism in the Holy Spirit:

Galatians 5:22-23 (NIV)
22 *But the fruit of the Spirit is love, joy, peace, patience, kindness, goodness, faithfulness,*
23 *gentleness and self-control. Against such things there is no law.*

We must keep in mind that it is the fruit **of the Spirit** and not the fruit of the individual person. We can't bear this fruit through human effort. It is the Holy Spirit who produces these virtues in us.

The supernatural gifts are also **of the Spirit**:

> 1 Corinthians 12:7-10
> 7 *But the manifestation of the Spirit is given to each one for the profit of all:*
> 8 *for to one is given the word of wisdom through the Spirit, to another the word of knowledge through the same Spirit,*
> 9 *to another faith by the same Spirit, to another gifts of healings by the same Spirit,*
> 10 *to another the working of miracles, to another prophecy, to another discerning of spirits, to another different kinds of tongues, to another the interpretation of tongues.*

When we receive the Holy Spirit, we receive more power to be like Jesus and to do His work.

(4) Didn't I receive the Holy Spirit when I was saved?

Yes. At salvation, we receive the Holy Spirit. In addition, it is the Holy Spirit who convicts us of sin (John 16:8), and it is the Holy Spirit who reveals to us that Jesus is the Savior (1 Corinthians 12:3).

When we are saved, the Holy Spirit "takes up residence" within us:

> 1 Corinthians 3:16
> *Do you not know that you are the temple of God and that the* ***Spirit of God dwells in you****?*

However, when Christians receive the **baptism** in the Holy Spirit, they receive additional power that enables them to carry out the Lord's ministry. Salvation involves **saving** the non-believer; Spirit baptism involves **empowering** the believer (Acts 1:8).

(5) If God wants me to have the baptism in the Holy Spirit, why doesn't He just "pour it on me"?

At times God moves in a sovereign way upon people, but usually the individual's will is involved. God rewards those who seek Him (Hebrews 11:6).

In 1 Corinthians 14:1, believers in Christ are specifically commanded to "earnestly desire spiritual gifts." Those who truly hunger for more of God and are sincerely seeking Him and His gifts receive more readily.

God makes all His gifts and blessings available to all, but He does not force anything on anyone. He does not **make** us get saved, or get healed, or get baptized in the Holy Spirit. We should want these blessings. Jesus instructed His disciples to **ask**:

> Luke 11:9-13
> 9 *"So I say to you, **ask**, and it will be given to you; seek, and you will find; knock, and it will be opened to you.*
> 10 *For everyone who **asks** receives, and he who seeks finds, and to him who knocks it will be opened.*
> 11 *If a son asks for bread from any father among you, will he give him a stone? Or if he asks for a fish, will he give him a serpent instead of a fish?*
> 12 *Or if he asks for an egg, will he offer him a scorpion?*

13 *If you then, being evil, know how to give good gifts to your children, how much more will your heavenly Father give the Holy Spirit to those who* ***ask*** *Him!"*

Did you notice the word "everyone" in verse 10? The blessings of the Lord are there for everyone, but we must ask, believe, and receive.

(6) How can I receive the baptism in the Holy Spirit since I don't feel worthy?

Some people do not feel "holy" enough to receive the Holy Spirit. If this is a concern, there are three things that must be understood.

First, the baptism in the Holy Spirit, like salvation, is a gift. We do not earn or deserve it:

Acts 10:45 (NIV)
The circumcised believers who had come with Peter were astonished that the ***gift*** *of the Holy Spirit had been poured out even on the Gentiles.*

Second, if you are a born-again believer, the blood of Jesus has cleansed you from sin. Because of His sacrifice, you have been made righteous. You are therefore worthy to receive the infilling of the Holy Spirit and all of God's other blessings:

2 Corinthians 5:21
For He made Him who knew no sin to be sin for us, that we might become the righteousness of God in Him.

> Ephesians 1:7
> *In Him we have redemption through His blood, the forgiveness of sins, according to the riches of His grace.*

Third, we need the power of the Holy Spirit to enable us to change. We cannot sanctify ourselves without the help of the Holy Spirit. The term "sanctification" literally means "being made holy." It is the ongoing process of the work of the Spirit in the life of the believer:

> 2 Thessalonians 2:13
> *But we are bound to give thanks to God always for you, brethren beloved by the Lord, because God from the beginning chose you for salvation through* ***sanctification by the Spirit*** *and belief in the truth.*

Believers are being gradually transformed into the image of Christ. Through sanctification we are becoming more and more like Him:

> 2 Corinthians 3:18
> *But we all, with unveiled face, beholding as in a mirror the glory of the Lord, are being transformed into the same image from glory to glory, just as by the Spirit of the Lord.*

However, unconfessed sin can separate us from God and hinder us from receiving His Holy Spirit. Therefore, if we are aware of specific sins in our lives, we must repent, confess the sin, and receive forgiveness and cleansing through the blood of Jesus:

> 1 John 1:9
> *If we confess our sins, He is faithful and just to forgive us our sins and to cleanse us from all unrighteousness.*

(7) Is it scriptural to tarry (wait) to receive the baptism in the Holy Spirit?

Some people have thought that since Jesus told His disciples to "tarry in Jerusalem," that tarrying is a prerequisite to receiving the Holy Spirit:

> Luke 24:49
> *"Behold, I send the Promise of My Father upon you; but tarry in the city of Jerusalem until you are endued with power from on high."*

The reason Jesus told His disciples to wait in Jerusalem was that He had to go to heaven first, in order for the Holy Spirit to come to earth. But now Jesus is already in heaven, and the Holy Spirit has already been given.

Since the day of Pentecost, when the Holy Spirit was first poured out, we find no instructions from the Lord directing anyone to wait in order to receive the baptism in the Holy Spirit. We do not have to wait, but we do have to desire more of the Lord and His power.

The disciples waited because the Holy Spirit had not yet been given, but, praise God, He is now here!

(8) What changes normally take place after Holy Spirit baptism?

The baptism in the Holy Spirit is a life-changing experience. We notice positive changes in our attitudes, in our behavior, in every aspect of our Christian walk—and others soon notice these changes, too.

For one thing, we feel closer to the Lord. The fruit of the Spirit is more evident in our lives. God may enable us to minister to others using His spiritual gifts. There is a greater interest in spiritual things. The Bible is easier to read and understand, and at times verses seem to come alive to us. We have more love and compassion for people. We are more motivated to pray, and when we do, we have more faith. We feel less intimidated about speaking out about our faith, and we are glad to share our testimony, because we want others to come into the joy we have found. The "still, small voice" of the Holy Spirit is easier to recognize as He leads and guides us. And one of the greatest blessings is an increased awareness of the Lord's presence throughout the day.

(9) How can someone who claims to have been baptized in the Spirit still live an imperfect life?

Every Spirit-filled believer should live an exemplary Christian life, but at times we see individuals who do not measure up to the highest standards. This is regrettable, because it is not a good witness, and it does not glorify the Lord.

We must keep in mind that there are different levels of spiritual maturity, and all of us have areas in which we have not yet been perfected. We receive God's blessings because we believe, not because we deserve them. We need the Holy Spirit to empower us to overcome our weaknesses. After all, if we were already perfect, we would not need the Holy Spirit.

Remember that we are saved by grace, and we live by grace. God's grace is one of the most wonderful aspects of

His divine nature. All of His precious gifts are given to us by grace, and once they are given they are not taken away (Romans 11:29).

Salvation is instantaneous, but sanctification is an ongoing process, and it takes time and the work of the Holy Spirit to complete the transformation within us:

> 2 Corinthians 3:18
> *But we all, with unveiled face, beholding as in a mirror the glory of the Lord, are being transformed into the same image from glory to glory, just as by the Spirit of the Lord.*

The validity of the baptism in the Holy Spirit should not be questioned on the basis of one person's immaturity. The genuineness of this experience should not be doubted or rejected because of someone's poor witness.

(10) What usually happens when one is baptized in the Holy Spirit?

There is no set pattern that applies to all, because God ministers uniquely to each individual, and people respond to God's touch in various ways. Many receive the baptism in the Holy Spirit quietly—in a very gentle, peaceful way. Others, when they come into contact with the power of the Spirit, may experience joy and laughter, or tears and weeping. Sometimes people tremble, or feel heat or a sensation like electricity. Occasionally, when the power of God comes upon an individual, he may not be able to stand, and he may "fall under the power," which is also called being "slain in the Spirit." On the day of Pentecost the crowd thought the Spirit-filled believers were drunk (Acts 2:13-15).

Still the most distinctive initial manifestation of the baptism in the Spirit—and the predominant one in Scripture—is speaking in tongues. This is such an important blessing that we will discuss it in detail in the next section.

SPEAKING IN TONGUES

"Speaking in tongues" is a term used in the Bible to refer to supernatural speech inspired by the Holy Spirit in languages never learned or intellectually understood by the speaker. Speaking in tongues has nothing to do with human linguistic aptitude, because the individual is not formulating the words, but rather voicing what the Holy Spirit gives him.

Since we speak several languages and also speak in tongues, we know first hand that learning a foreign language and speaking in tongues are two entirely different things. It takes time and effort to learn a foreign language; however, speaking in tongues is not intellectually learned. When a believer speaks in tongues, he is not bound by natural or intellectual limitations. He yields his speech organs to the leading of the Spirit, giving voice to whatever prayer, praise, or utterance He directs.

Speaking in tongues is one of the main signs or manifestations of being baptized in the Holy Spirit. It is **not** the baptism in the Holy Spirit—it is what happens when individuals are baptized in the Spirit. Several times in the New Testament, individuals spoke in tongues when the Holy Spirit came upon them:

> Acts 2:4
> *And they were all filled with the Holy Spirit and began to speak with other tongues, as the Spirit gave them utterance.*

Acts 10:46
For they heard them speak with tongues and magnify God...

Acts 19:6
And when Paul had laid hands on them, the Holy Spirit came upon them, and they spoke with tongues and prophesied.

Before His ascension, Jesus underscored the importance of this gift, saying that it is one of the five supernatural signs that would follow believers:

Mark 16:17-18
17 *"And these signs will follow those who believe: In My name they will cast out demons;* ***they will speak with new tongues****;*
18 *they will take up serpents; and if they drink anything deadly, it will by no means hurt them; they will lay hands on the sick, and they will recover."*

The Apostle Paul also emphasized the importance of speaking in tongues and stated that he spoke in tongues often. In fact, in speaking to the Corinthians, he said that he did so more than any of them, and he encouraged all of the believers there to speak in tongues also:

1 Corinthians 14:5
I wish you all spoke with tongues...

1 Corinthians 14:18
I thank my God I speak with tongues more than you all.

The Uses of Tongues

There are two main ways that tongues are used: the personal use, and the public use.

(1) Tongues for Personal Use

The most frequent use of tongues is as a prayer language. This is a devotional language for private use. Speaking in tongues is prayer with or in the spirit. It is the individual's spirit speaking to God in an unknown language, as led by the Holy Spirit. This is what Paul was making reference to in 1 Corinthians 14:

> 1 Corinthians 14:14
> *For if I pray in a tongue, my spirit prays, but my understanding is unfruitful.*

Speaking in tongues takes place when a believer speaks to God, but instead of speaking in a language that he knows with his intellect, he just speaks by faith from the heart, trusting the Holy Spirit to provide the unknown words.

In other words, the regenerated human spirit, in union with the Holy Spirit, communicates to God in a new language that is pure, supernatural, and not limited by the human mind.

Speaking in tongues is **not** the Holy Spirit speaking. It's **you**. It's your mouth and your vocal chords making the sounds, as led by the Holy Spirit:

> Acts 2:4 (NIV)
> *All of them were filled with the Holy Spirit and began to speak in other tongues as the Spirit enabled them.*

1 Corinthians 14:15
What is the conclusion then? I will pray with the spirit, and I will also pray with the understanding. I will sing with the spirit, and I will also sing with the understanding.

These and other biblical passages show us that it is man who speaks in tongues, as the Spirit enables. Note that these Scriptures say, "All of them ... began to speak," and, "I will pray with the spirit."

The person's will is involved. God does not **make** a person pray in tongues any more than He makes him pray with his understanding. The Holy Spirit inspires us to pray, but He does not make us. The believer still has control, and he decides when to speak, how fast, how loud, how long, etc. The Holy Spirit is the Helper. This is a wondrous union. When we pray in the spirit, the Holy Spirit prays through us. It's not just us, but it's not just the Holy Spirit either. We speak as He enables us. The individual is speaking directly to God in his spirit:

1 Corinthians 14:2
For he who speaks in a tongue does not speak to men but to God...

Since the believer is speaking to God and not to man, this use of tongues does not have to be interpreted. After all, God understands all languages. However, at times the Lord may give an individual the interpretation of his own personal prayer, or he may have a sensing of what he is praying about.

Believers may also use tongues to sing in the spirit. The Apostle Paul stated that he could pray in the spirit and sing in the spirit:

1 Corinthians 14:15
What is the conclusion then? I will pray with the spirit, and I will also pray with the understanding. ***I will sing*** *with the spirit, and I will also sing with the understanding.*

Note that the believer is not to pray in tongues exclusively. Believers should pray both in tongues and in their learned language. If one is bilingual or multilingual, he can pray in two or more languages as he chooses, but this is not the same as praying "in tongues." Praying both in the spirit and in a known language enhances our prayer. This personal communication can at times take place in a corporate setting (for example, group prayer or singing in the spirit), whether it is together with other believers or individually in quiet prayer.

(2) Tongues for Public Use

The second way that tongues may be used is in a public setting, when an individual is directed by the Holy Spirit to communicate God's message to everyone present. This is called the "gift of tongues." It is one of the nine gifts of the Holy Spirit (1 Corinthians 12:8-10). Since all hear this unknown tongue, it must be interpreted into the known language, so the listeners can benefit:

1 Corinthians 14:26-28
26 *How is it then, brethren? Whenever you come together, each of you has a psalm, has a teaching, has a tongue, has a revelation, has an interpretation. Let all things be done for edification.*
27 *If anyone speaks in a tongue, let there be two or at the most three, each in turn, and let one interpret.*
28 *But if there is no interpreter, let him keep silent in church, and let him speak to himself and to God.*

Our experience has shown that a "tongue" may be God speaking to people, or it may be a public prayer, praise, or thanksgiving. Either way, it must be interpreted:

> 1 Corinthians 14:16-17 (NIV)
> 16 *If you are praising God with your spirit, how can one who finds himself among those who do not understand say "Amen" to your thanksgiving, since he does not know what you are saying?*
> 17 *You may be giving thanks well enough, but the other man is not edified.*

One may not realize that in chapter 14 Paul is discussing both the private and the public use of tongues. As a result, it may not be clear at first which one the apostle is referring to. Notice how he alternates between the two uses of tongues in these verses:

> 1 Corinthians 14:1-5
> 1 *Pursue love, and desire spiritual gifts, but especially that you may prophesy.*
> 2 *For he who speaks in a tongue does not speak to men but to God, for no one understands him; however, in the spirit he speaks mysteries.*
> 3 *But he who prophesies speaks edification and exhortation and comfort to men.*
> 4 *He who speaks in a tongue edifies himself, but he who prophesies edifies the church.*
> 5 *I wish you all spoke with tongues, but even more that you prophesied; for he who prophesies is greater than he who speaks with tongues, unless indeed he interprets, that the church may receive edification.*

In verses 2 and 4, Paul is explaining the use of tongues as a personal prayer language. At the end of verse 5, he is referring to the public use of the gift of tongues with interpretation. We will discuss this in the next section.

THE GIFT OF INTERPRETATION OF TONGUES

The gift of interpretation of tongues refers to a believer's declaring by the inspiration of the Holy Spirit the meaning of what was said in an unknown language. As we have seen, this is one of the nine gifts of the Holy Spirit listed in 1 Corinthians 12:8-10.

This gift is to follow the gift of tongues when given at a Christian gathering, so that those present will know what was said in the unknown language. This is different from private prayer in tongues, which does not have to be interpreted. Praying in tongues privately without interpretation edifies the individual (1 Corinthians 14:4). Like prophecy, the gift of tongues with interpretation at a group meeting edifies the church (1 Corinthians 14:5).

The Apostle Paul gave the Christians in Corinth guidelines on the proper use of these gifts:

> 1 Corinthians 14:26-28
> 26 *How is it then, brethren? Whenever you come together, each of you has a psalm, has a teaching, has a tongue, has a revelation, has an interpretation. Let all things be done for edification.*
> 27 *If anyone speaks in a tongue, let there be two or at the most three, each in turn, and let one interpret.*
> 28 *But if there is no interpreter, let him keep silent in church, and let him speak to himself and to God.*

From reading this and other passages, we learn that Paul did not forbid or discourage these gifts. On the contrary, he expected the gifts of tongues and interpretation of tongues to be normal components of a congregational meeting. He says that when believers get together, everyone will have something to contribute to the meeting, and he lists several things, including the gifts of tongues and interpretation. These gifts, then, were expected to be in operation under the leading of the Holy Spirit. Paul is emphasizing the importance of interpreting the gift of tongues in a public meeting, so that the hearers may understand what was said and benefit from it.

This explanation and context also apply to verse 23:

> 1 Corinthians 14:23 (NIV)
> *So if the whole church comes together and everyone speaks in tongues, and some who do not understand or some unbelievers come in, will they not say that you are out of your mind?*

Some interpret this verse to mean that tongues should not be used publicly in order to avoid offending people. However if we read on through verse 33, we see Paul giving guidance on how to flow in the Holy Spirit in an orderly way so that individuals will not be "turned off" but sense God's presence and worship Him. He admonished that in addition to the other gifts, there should be only two or three "tongues," given one at a time, and that they should be interpreted so that everyone may be instructed and encouraged.

We should point out that interpretation is not the same as translation. The individual who is prompted and anointed by the Holy Spirit to interpret a message in tongues is not giving a word for word translation, but rather the interpretation or meaning of what was said. The individual giving the interpretation has no intellectual knowledge of the "tongue" that he heard, but by the inspiration of the Holy Spirit he has a "knowing" of what was said, and by faith he steps out and gives the general meaning. If two individuals were to interpret the same utterance, their wording would be slightly different, because people have differing speech patterns and other unique characteristics, but the general meaning would be the same.

Any Spirit-baptized Christian should desire and be ready to exercise these gifts. Here are some practical suggestions to keep in mind: if you feel the anointing come over you, and you know that the leadership of the group allows the operation of the gifts, ask the Lord to give you a confirmation and the timing. Once you give the utterance in tongues, pray quietly for the right interpretation to be given, and give others present an opportunity to give it (1 Corinthians 12:10). However, if no one else does, be ready to interpret it yourself (1 Corinthians 14:13). If you are receiving the interpretation, and someone else gives a similar message, you do not need to give yours also.

The interpretation may come through a mental picture, a Scripture, or simply through inspired thoughts. Not only should the content of the interpretation be in line with the written Word of God, but it should express the heart and nature of God. The manner of delivery is also very important. Shouting, an unusual tone of voice, or too much emotionalism can weaken the impact of the gift.

Although we desire to excel in the operation of these gifts, we should not allow the fear of making a mistake to hold us back from speaking out. Through practice and correction, if necessary, we will develop our gifts.

The gift of tongues, the gift of interpretation of tongues, and all the other gifts of the Holy Spirit, are essential for strengthening and increasing the body of believers.

BENEFITS OF SPEAKING IN TONGUES

Everything that our heavenly Father gives us is a wonderful gift. James uses the adjectives "good" and "perfect" to describe God's gifts:

> James 1:17
> *Every **good** gift and every **perfect** gift is from above, and comes down from the Father of lights, with whom there is no variation or shadow of turning.*

The Holy Spirit Himself is a good Gift:

> Acts 2:38 (NIV)
> *Peter replied, "Repent and be baptized, every one of you, in the name of Jesus Christ for the forgiveness of your sins. And you will receive the **gift** of the Holy Spirit."*

> Acts 10:45 (NIV)
> *The circumcised believers who had come with Peter were astonished that the **gift** of the Holy Spirit had been poured out even on the Gentiles.*

Speaking in tongues is one of those special gifts the Father has given to His children. The Apostle Paul was certainly grateful to have this gift:

> 1 Corinthians 14:18
> *I thank my God I speak with tongues more than you all.*

There are many benefits to speaking in tongues. Let's look at some of them:

(1) Speaking in tongues is an added confirmation that one is a believer.

Mark 16:17-18
17 *"And these signs will follow* ***those who believe****: In My name they will cast out demons; they will speak with new tongues;*
18 *they will take up serpents; and if they drink anything deadly, it will by no means hurt them; they will lay hands on the sick, and they will recover."*

Jesus said that all five of these signs would accompany believers. Speaking in tongues is an added confirmation to the individual that he is one of "those who believe."

(2) Speaking in tongues is a sign or evidence of the indwelling presence of the Holy Spirit.

Since speaking in other tongues is one of the primary signs of the baptism in the Holy Spirit, when an individual speaks in other tongues, he is reassured that he has indeed been baptized in the Spirit:

Acts 2:4 (NIV)
All of them were filled with the Holy Spirit and began to speak in other tongues as the Spirit enabled them.

Acts 19:6
And when Paul had laid hands on them, the Holy Spirit came upon them, and they spoke with tongues and prophesied.

Acts 10:45-46 (NASB)
45 *All the circumcised believers who came with Peter were amazed, because the gift of the Holy Spirit*

> *had been poured out on the Gentiles also.*
> 46 *For they were hearing them speaking with tongues and exalting God...*

How did Peter and the Jews with him know that the Holy Spirit had been poured out even on the Gentiles? Verse 46 tells us that they heard them speaking in tongues. About a decade after the Holy Spirit had been poured out upon the 120 in the Upper Room in Jerusalem and they had spoken in tongues, speaking in tongues was still a sign that believers recognized and accepted as evidence that an individual had received the baptism in the Holy Spirit.

In Acts 11 Peter reported what had happened at Cornelius' house:

> Acts 11:15-16
> 15 *"And as I began to speak, the Holy Spirit fell upon them, as upon us at the beginning.*
> 16 *Then I remembered the word of the Lord, how He said, 'John indeed baptized with water, but you shall be baptized with the Holy Spirit.'"*

Peter did not have to wonder if or assume that the Holy Spirit had been poured out on the Gentiles. He knew they had received, for he heard them speaking in tongues.

Several years later, Paul prayed for twelve men in Ephesus, and they also received the Holy Spirit and spoke in tongues (Acts 19:1-7).

Thank God that this experience was not just for the Jews, but also for the Gentiles; and not only for the early church, but for all (Acts 2:16-18).

(3) Speaking in tongues is a supernatural way to control the tongue.

Another benefit of speaking in tongues is found in the epistle of James. Here the apostle talks about the carnal use of the tongue (the speech organ):

> James 3:8-9 (NIV)
> 8 *but no man can tame the tongue. It is a restless evil, full of deadly poison.*
> 9 *With the tongue we praise our Lord and Father, and with it we curse men, who have been made in God's likeness.*

The Apostle James says that no man can tame the tongue. Because of our human nature, we can say evil things, sometimes without thinking. When we speak in tongues, the Holy Spirit guides the tongue, and He will not say anything that will displease God. Whenever we speak in tongues, we are speaking a holy language.

(4) Speaking in tongues enables the believer to praise and worship God in an unlimited way.

Jesus said that we are to worship the Father in spirit and in truth:

> John 4:24
> *"God is Spirit, and those who worship Him must worship in spirit and truth."*

Speaking in tongues enables us to praise and worship God in the dimension of the spirit. When the outpouring occurred in Acts 2, the visitors present for the feast heard and understood the tongues, and they reported that these believers were praising and worshiping God:

Acts 2:11
"...we hear them speaking in our own tongues the wonderful works of God."

Acts 10:46 (NASB)
For they were hearing them speaking with tongues and exalting God...

Speaking in tongues enhances one's ability to praise and worship God. Believers can thank God for specific blessings with their minds, yet they don't always know how to adequately praise and magnify God for who He is.

But as one yields to the Spirit and speaks in tongues, there rises from within him a new dimension of love, adoration, and awe for the Lord without any limitation.

Of course, praising God in tongues should not replace praising Him with the understanding, but rather it should supplement it. The Apostle Paul makes this clear in his first letter to the Corinthians:

1 Corinthians 14:15
What is the conclusion then? I will pray with the spirit, and I will also pray with the understanding. I will sing with the spirit, and I will also sing with the understanding.

(5) Speaking in tongues is a supernatural means of communicating with God.

Speaking in tongues is not only a powerful vehicle of praise, but also of prayer:

1 Corinthians 14:2
For he who speaks in a tongue does not speak to men

but to God, for no one understands him; however, in the spirit he speaks mysteries.

This verse tells us that he who speaks in tongues is speaking to God, and that in the spirit he is praying mysteries or secrets. As the Holy Spirit leads, the believer is by faith declaring things that are unknown to him by the intellect. There is therefore no limit as to what he can pray.

Praying in tongues is especially valuable in times of decision, difficulty, or perplexity. With the help of the Holy Spirit, we can pray exactly what needs to be prayed at the moment, and with less effort and concentration on our part.

(6) Speaking in tongues helps us pray correctly.

James tells us that we do not always get results from our prayers because we do not pray correctly:

James 4:3 (NIV)
When you ask, you do not receive, because you ask with wrong motives, that you may spend what you get on your pleasures.

But when we pray in tongues, it is not just our mind (soul) that prays, but the Holy Spirit, and He is always right, because He prays according to God's will:

Romans 8:27
Now He who searches the hearts knows what the mind of the Spirit is, because He makes intercession for the saints ***according to the will of God****.*

The Bible further tells us that prayers which are prayed in accordance with God's will are effective prayers:

> 1 John 5:14-15
> 14 *Now this is the confidence that we have in Him, that if we ask anything according to His will, He hears us.*
> 15 *And if we know that He hears us, whatever we ask, we know that we have the petitions that we have asked of Him.*

Since the Holy Spirit prays according to the will of God, we can be confident that every prayer we pray in tongues will be answered.

Speaking in tongues is God's marvelous provision that enables the believer to pray effectively.

(7) Speaking in tongues helps us intercede for others.

We need the Holy Spirit's help to pray for others:

> Romans 8:26-27
> 26 *Likewise the Spirit also helps in our weaknesses. For we do not know what we should pray for as we ought, but the Spirit Himself makes intercession for us with groanings which cannot be uttered.*
> 27 *Now He who searches the hearts knows what the mind of the Spirit is, because He* ***makes intercession for the saints*** *according to the will of God.*

As this passage says, we do not always know what to pray or how to pray "as we ought." But even when in our own minds we do not know what to ask for in prayer, we can pray in tongues and it will be exactly right.

Verse 27 tells us that the Spirit intercedes for the saints (prays for other Christians) in accordance with the will of God. When we pray in tongues, it is our spirit praying by the Holy Spirit within us. We do the speaking, but the Holy Spirit does the directing. We pray in tongues as He gives us the utterance, so whatever we are saying is in harmony with God's will. This is Spirit-led prayer, so it eliminates the possibility of praying incorrectly, since the prayer is not created in our minds.

Of course, Spirit-led praying is not limited to praying in tongues, but would include any prayer that is inspired by the Holy Spirit—whether it is voiced in a known or an unknown language. But as we saw in James 4:3, not all prayers spoken in our learned language are Spirit-led. By contrast, all prayers prayed in tongues are Spirit-led, since they bypass the mind.

The Bible says that when we pray in tongues our minds are unproductive:

> 1 Corinthians 14:14
> *For if I pray in a tongue, my spirit prays, but my understanding is unfruitful.*

So praying in tongues is a wonderful tool to use when we intercede for others. The Holy Spirit, who knows everything, can pray through us for things we know nothing about with our natural minds. The Spirit knows exactly what to pray for and can pray specifically and concisely. We can be sure that these prayers are powerful and effective.

(8) Speaking in tongues edifies the believer.

Praying in tongues is a powerful way to strengthen and edify yourself spiritually. This is another benefit noted by Paul:

> 1 Corinthians 14:4
> *He who speaks in a tongue edifies himself, but he who prophesies edifies the church.*

The verb "edify" means to "build up." Another meaning for this word is to "charge."

Every Christian needs to be charged up and built up.

Jude tells us that praying in tongues energizes our faith:

> Jude 20
> *But you, beloved, building yourselves up on your most holy faith, praying in the Holy Spirit...*

Praying in tongues stimulates faith, and in the process we learn to trust God more.

As we pray in tongues, God's power flows into our lives, giving us peace, joy, courage, faith, and hope to face the challenges of life. As we communicate with God in this supernatural way, we are aware of His presence and we are refreshed, revived, restored, and refilled:

> John 7:37-39
> 37 *On the last day, that great day of the feast, Jesus stood and cried out, saying, "If anyone thirsts, let him come to Me and drink.*
> 38 *He who believes in Me, as the Scripture has said, out of his heart will flow rivers of living water."*

> 39 *But this He spoke concerning the Spirit, whom those believing in Him would receive; for the Holy Spirit was not yet given, because Jesus was not yet glorified.*

May those rivers of living water flow freely out of us—cleansing, healing, and empowering us.

(9) The gift of tongues edifies other believers also.

Not only is an individual edified when he prays in his prayer language, but when the gifts of tongues and interpretation are used in a corporate setting, the believers present are blessed:

> 1 Corinthians 14:26
> *How is it then, brethren? Whenever you come together, each of you has a psalm, has a teaching, has a tongue, has a revelation, has an interpretation. Let all things be done for edification.*

> 1 Corinthians 14:5
> *I wish you all spoke with tongues, but even more that you prophesied; for he who prophesies is greater than he who speaks with tongues, unless indeed he interprets, that the church may receive edification.*

When the Holy Spirit uses someone to give a message in tongues (the gift of tongues), and that gift is followed by an interpretation, this edifies the hearers. The combination of these two gifts has an effect much like the gift of prophecy, in that everyone hears and understands what was said and is edified.

(10) Tongues are a sign to unbelievers.

The gift of tongues can also be a blessing to non-Christians:

> 1 Corinthians 14:22
> *Therefore tongues are for a sign, not to those who believe but to unbelievers...*

At times, the Holy Spirit will speak through "tongues" to an unbeliever in a language he knows or understands. The one speaking in tongues has no knowledge of that language, but the one hearing understands what is said and that message becomes a convincing "sign" to him.

We remember hearing a testimony years ago from evangelist A. G. Dornfeld that confirms this. He shared that in one of his meetings a Spirit-filled lady gave a message in tongues. She did not know what language she was speaking, but a Jewish lady who was visiting that day recognized the "tongue" as Hebrew. The interpretation, given by someone else, was something like this: "As I spoke through the prophets, so I am speaking to you today, my child..." Since the Jewish lady understood the "tongue," she said with amazement that the language was Hebrew, and she confirmed that the interpretation given was the true meaning of the message. Later she came back and wanted to talk to the evangelist about Jesus. When the Spirit-filled woman gave that message in tongues, it became a sign to this unbeliever. She was then ready to hear more about Jesus.

The speaking in other tongues by the newly Spirit-baptized believers on the day of Pentecost was also a sign to those who had gathered in Jerusalem for the feast.

These visitors were Jews who lived in foreign lands and who had come to Jerusalem to take part in the religious festival. When they heard those Galileans speaking in languages they understood, they were amazed. Hearing them speaking in tongues was a sign from heaven, for they heard them praising God in languages they had not learned. The listeners knew that those Spirit-filled believers did not know what they were saying, and this was proof of the miraculous nature of this event.

Actually, there were three supernatural signs present at this occasion: first, “a sound from heaven, as of a rushing mighty wind,” second, “divided tongues, as of fire,” and third, “other tongues” (Acts 2:1-4). Each of these signs had a part in preparing the people to receive the Gospel of Christ, but they were so astonished by the phenomenon of speaking in tongues that this topic dominated their conversations (verses 5-13). So when Peter seized the opportunity and boldly addressed the crowd, they were ready to hear his message, and as a result 3,000 people were saved that day (verses 14-41).

Even if visitors do not understand the language used in a service, hearing believers speaking in a supernatural language may cause those individuals to sense the anointing and the presence of God. This may convince them of the reality of the Lord and give them a hunger for spiritual things.

These are just some of the benefits of speaking in tongues. For these and other reasons, we should really **want** to step into this new dimension in the Spirit. Praying in tongues is a wonderful way to stay refreshed and built up. Not only does the Holy Spirit fill us, but He overflows from us to bless others.

SOME COMMON QUESTIONS ABOUT TONGUES

(1) Aren't tongues the least important gift?

Paul listed tongues and interpretation of tongues at the end of the nine gifts of the Holy Spirit in 1 Corinthians 12, but this does not mean that they are inferior to the other gifts:

> 1 Corinthians 12:8-10
> 8 *for to one is given the word of wisdom through the Spirit, to another the word of knowledge through the same Spirit,*
> 9 *to another faith by the same Spirit, to another gifts of healings by the same Spirit,*
> 10 *to another the working of miracles, to another prophecy, to another discerning of spirits, to another different kinds of tongues, to another the interpretation of tongues.*

If one says that tongues and interpretation are the least important gifts because they are listed last, then by the same reasoning love is the least important virtue, since it's also listed last in 1 Corinthians 13:

> 1 Corinthians 13:13
> *And now abide faith, hope, love, these three; but the greatest of these is love.*

All the gifts of the Spirit are supernatural, and all are very important.

(2) Isn't it true that tongues have ceased?

No, tongues and the gifts of the Holy Spirit have not ceased. They are for all believers, even today.

People who think that tongues have ceased sometimes use 1 Corinthians 13:8-10 to justify their thinking:

> 1 Corinthians 13:8-10
> 8 *Love never fails. But whether there are prophecies, they will fail; whether there are tongues, they will cease; whether there is knowledge, it will vanish away.*
> 9 *For we know in part and we prophesy in part.*
> 10 *But when that which is perfect has come, then that which is in part will be done away.*

Some say that "that which is perfect" (verse 10) refers to the New Testament. They reason that since we now have the complete Bible, we do not need tongues any longer. However, the context of this passage, which includes verse 12, discredits this idea:

> 1 Corinthians 13:12 (NIV)
> *Now we see but a poor reflection as in a mirror; then we shall see face to face. Now I know in part; then I shall know fully, even as I am fully known.*

"That which is perfect" will come when Jesus returns and we see Him face to face. At that time the three things listed in verse 8—prophecy, tongues, and knowledge—will cease. If prophecy and tongues have ceased, then it must also be true that knowledge has ceased, since they are all listed together. But knowledge has certainly not ceased. It has increased. Prophecy and tongues have not ended either. They will all pass away when Jesus Christ returns. When He returns, we will clearly see and know Him (1 John 3:2). At that time, we can expect prophecy, tongues, and knowledge to be superseded.

(3) What about the verse that says, "Do all speak in tongues?"

Some question whether speaking in tongues is for everyone. They use the passage in 1 Corinthians 12:27-30 to support their position:

> 1 Corinthians 12:27-30
> 27 *Now you are the body of Christ, and members individually.*
> 28 *And God has appointed these in the church: first apostles, second prophets, third teachers, after that miracles, then gifts of healings, helps, administrations, varieties of tongues.*
> 29 *Are all apostles? Are all prophets? Are all teachers? Are all workers of miracles?*
> 30 *Do all have gifts of healings? Do all speak with tongues? Do all interpret?*

The answer implied here is **no**. Not everyone will speak in tongues at a public meeting, just as not everyone will teach or preach, etc.

Paul is speaking here about a ministry gift. He is not talking about being filled with the Holy Spirit and speaking in tongues for personal devotions.

(4) Do I have to speak in tongues?

No, you do not have to speak in tongues in order to be a Christian, or to go to heaven, or to have the Holy Spirit working in your life. But if you want to experience the energizing power of the Holy Spirit working in you and through you, you will want to receive this precious gift.

People who ask, "Do I have to speak in tongues" usually are not informed about the benefits of speaking in tongues. It should not be "Do I have to?" but "Do I get to?" It is a privilege.

As we saw in the previous chapter, there are many benefits of speaking in tongues. It is a powerful way to communicate with God and to be strengthened, refreshed, and recharged.

(5) Did Jesus speak in tongues?

There is no record in the Bible of Jesus speaking in tongues; however, it is very clear that He advocated it. It was Jesus who said that speaking in tongues would be a sign that would follow believers:

> Mark 16:17-18
> 17 *"And these signs will follow those who believe: In My name they will cast out demons;* ***they will speak with new tongues****;*
> 18 *they will take up serpents; and if they drink anything deadly, it will by no means hurt them; they will lay hands on the sick, and they will recover."*

(6) What if I get the wrong thing?

Some people are reluctant to speak in tongues for fear that they will receive something from the devil, or that they will create something in their own minds.

We can certainly appreciate the desire to receive only what is pure and authentic, but you should not allow fear or doubt to keep you from receiving all that God has for you. Consider the very comforting promise that Jesus made in the Gospel of Luke:

> Luke 11:9-13
> 9 *"So I say to you, ask, and it will be given to you; seek, and you will find; knock, and it will be opened to you.*
> 10 *For everyone who asks receives, and he who seeks finds, and to him who knocks it will be opened.*
> 11 *If a son asks for bread from any father among you, will he give him a stone? Or if he asks for a fish, will he give him a serpent instead of a fish?*
> 12 *Or if he asks for an egg, will he offer him a scorpion?*
> 13 *If you then, being evil, know how to give good gifts to your children, how much more will your heavenly Father give the Holy Spirit to those who ask Him!"*

This passage reassures us that it will not be the devil, but God who will give the Holy Spirit to His children. In fact, praying in tongues is a powerful weapon against the devil.

When we ask in the name of Jesus, what we receive will be from God, and not a counterfeit. He is more eager to give us His precious gifts than we are to receive them. So ask in faith, trusting that you will receive a good gift.

(7) How often should one speak in tongues?

A Spirit-baptized believer can speak in his personal prayer language whenever he chooses. We should pray daily, both in the spirit and with the intellect.

Paul prayed in tongues a lot:

> 1 Corinthians 14:18
> *I thank my God I speak with tongues more than you all.*

But at a public gathering, it is the Holy Spirit who directs who should speak in tongues and when. In his devotional time, the believer prays in tongues as **he** wills; however, in a public setting, the believer speaks in tongues only as the **Spirit** wills.

Like all the gifts of the Spirit, the gift of tongues and the gift of interpretation of tongues are to be exercised under the leading of the Holy Spirit:

> 1 Corinthians 12:11
> *But one and the same Spirit works all these things, distributing to each one individually as He wills.*

One must keep in mind that, as with any of the gifts, their use must be in a setting where the church leadership encourages their operation (Hebrews 13:17).

(8) Does my speaking in tongues need to be interpreted?

Your prayer language does not need to be interpreted. Even though you may not know what you are saying, usually you have a sensing of what you are praying about. You are speaking to God and not to men. God understands every language, so you do not need to interpret for Him:

> 1 Corinthians 14:2
> *For he who speaks in a tongue does not speak to men*

but to God, for no one understands him; however, in the spirit he speaks mysteries.

But if the Holy Spirit directs you to speak out loud in tongues at a public meeting, that "tongue" needs to be interpreted, so that those present can understand what is said. This would be the gift of tongues followed by the gift of interpretation of tongues.

This gift of tongues in a public setting is what Paul was referring to in the following verses:

1 Corinthians 14:5
I wish you all spoke with tongues, but even more that you prophesied; for he who prophesies is greater than he who speaks with tongues, unless indeed he interprets, that the church may receive edification.

1 Corinthians 14:27-28
27 *If anyone speaks in a tongue, let there be two or at the most three, each in turn, and let one interpret.*
28 *But if there is no interpreter, let him keep silent in church, and let him speak to himself and to God.*

(9) What is the point of speaking in tongues, since this sounds like nonsense to me?

To begin with, speaking in tongues is a supernatural phenomenon that was ordained by God. God Himself is supernatural, and His Spirit is supernatural—meaning above and beyond the natural mind.

We must keep in mind that when we pray in tongues, we don't speak to men, but to God. Paul says in 1 Corinthians 14:2 that we are speaking mysteries to God in the spirit. It is not nonsense to Him, for He knows all languages.

That these diversities of tongues are real, and not just "gibberish," has been verified by Scripture and by experience. On the day of Pentecost, when the 120 were baptized in the Spirit, they spoke in other tongues that many in the crowd were able to recognize. To the amazement of the crowd, the Galileans were speaking in languages that the hearers understood. The 120 newly Spirit-baptized believers spoke in at least fifteen different known languages that day (Acts 2:5-11).

Some think that the reason they spoke in these languages was to preach to those gathered there in Jerusalem for Pentecost. But verse 11 negates this idea, since they were not speaking to men, but praising God.

Tongues are actual languages and not just emotional babbling. This has been confirmed time and again by missionaries. We have had several people share with us unique experiences from the mission field. On one occasion some American friends, who were ministering in Venezuela, were at a prayer meeting. The believers there were praying in Spanish when a young lady with her eyes closed spoke out in English. Of course, our friends understood what she had said, but she had no idea that she had been speaking in English. After the prayer meeting, when the missionaries went over and spoke to her in English, the lady could not understand a word they were saying. That's when they realized that she had been speaking in tongues. This was not babbling. In this case, the unknown "tongue" was English.

A number of years ago, in a service at our former church in Missouri, a lady gave a message in tongues. The language was incomprehensible to us, but God gave me (Eva) the interpretation, which I spoke out in English, so that everyone could understand. A nine-year-old boy from India, who had been adopted by a couple in our church, was present at that service—in fact, he had just recently come to the United States. He recognized the "tongue" and turned to his adoptive mother, asking "Why are they speaking in Malayalam?" It was a language he knew from living in India. He confirmed that the "tongue" was a real language and that the interpretation given was correct. Needless to say, we were all blessed and encouraged by such a confirmation. This experience validated both the gift of tongues and the gift of interpretation.

There are more than 6,000 known languages on earth. Some of these are tonal languages, some involve a complex system of clicks, and some are spoken by very primitive tribes. Many of these would sound like nonsense to us, and yet they function well within their linguistic communities. In addition to all these earthly languages, or "tongues of men," the Apostle Paul makes reference to "tongues of angels" (1 Corinthians 13:1).

In summary, regardless of how tongues may sound, if they are inspired by the Holy Spirit they are indeed valuable.

(10) What if I want to speak in tongues, but I don't get a release, or I just get a few words?

If you only get a few words, continue to use those words to speak to the Father. Do not allow fear and doubt to stop you from pouring your heart out to the Lord. As you step out in faith, speaking to the Father in those few words, soon more words will be added, and before long your new language will be flowing freely.

After speaking in tongues for the first time, you, like many others, may think: "That was just me!" The truth is that it was indeed you: your lips, your tongue, your speech organs—not someone else's. But it was not **just** you. It was you speaking, but not with your intellect. The Holy Spirit gave you the words.

The union between the believer's speaking and the Holy Spirit's prompting is so mysterious that it is hard to draw a line between your speaking and His prompting. So the natural response is to think, "I am just making all this up." But do not let these thoughts cause you to draw back or deny your experience. Rather, let the authority of God's Word instill in you the confidence that what you are speaking is indeed a real language given to you by the Lord.

If you are not released right away in your prayer language, do not go away feeling defeated or disappointed. Remember that tongues are only one manifestation of the Spirit. Not speaking in tongues does not mean that you have not received the Holy Spirit and His power.

At times individuals receive their prayer language in their cars on their way home from a meeting, or in their sleep, or at some later time. So do not doubt your experience. Believe that you have received and you will (Mark 11:24).

RECEIVING FROM GOD

A powerful truth about enjoying the blessings of God is the principle that some biblical scholars refer to as the "law of appropriation."

Simply put, the law of appropriation is this: God gives, but man must take.

The verb "to appropriate" means to take or to take possession of. And the noun "appropriation" means taking for one's own use.

God has abundant blessings for all, but only those who reach out and take those blessings will experience a victorious life. God gives, but we must receive. Appropriating what He has for us takes an act of faith. We believe and we receive (Mark 11:24).

That word "receive" is found over and over in the Scriptures. It is such a common verb that we often fail to recognize its significance. Here are just a few of the blessings that God gives, and we must receive, by faith:

The Word of God

James 1:21
*...**receive** with meekness the implanted **word**, which is able to save your souls.*

Acts 8:14
*Now when the apostles who were at Jerusalem heard that Samaria had **received the word of God**, they sent Peter and John to them.*

Jesus

Motivated by His great love, God the Father gave His precious Son so that we can have eternal life:

John 3:16
"For God so loved the world that He ***gave*** *His only begotten Son, that whoever believes in Him should not perish but have everlasting life."*

But we must **receive** the Gift (Jesus) that God gave:

John 1:12
But as many as ***received Him****, to them He gave the right to become children of God, to those who believe in His name.*

The Holy Spirit

John 20:22
*And when He had said this, He breathed on them, and said to them, "****Receive the Holy Spirit.****"*

Acts 1:8
"But you shall ***receive*** *power when the Holy Spirit has come upon you; and you shall be witnesses to Me in Jerusalem, and in all Judea and Samaria, and to the end of the earth."*

Acts 8:17
Then they laid hands on them, and they ***received the Holy Spirit.***

Acts 10:47
"Can anyone forbid water, that these should not be baptized who have ***received the Holy Spirit*** *just as we have?"*

When we receive Jesus, His Word, and the Holy Spirit, we receive numerous other blessings. We receive God's love, His forgiveness, His grace, His power, His authority, His anointing, His healing, His joy, His peace, His wisdom, His ministry, etc.

In this book we have studied many Bible passages. It is our prayer that as you have read the written Word of God, the Holy Spirit has made Himself real to you, and you have a hunger for more of Him. We hope you have seen the importance of the empowerment of the Holy Spirit in fulfilling your calling. We really want you to experience the reality of His presence in your daily life, and the joy of seeing others ministered to, as His power flows through you.

God has POWER FOR ALL, but we must reach out and take it. The information in the next two sections will guide you in receiving salvation through Jesus Christ and the baptism in the Holy Spirit.

HOW TO BECOME A CHRISTIAN

(1) Admit you are a sinner.

Romans 3:10
As it is written: "There is none righteous, no, not one."

Romans 3:23
for all have sinned and fall short of the glory of God.

(2) Repent of your sin.

Acts 2:38
Then Peter said to them, "Repent, and let every one of you be baptized in the name of Jesus Christ for the remission of sins..."

1 John 1:9
If we confess our sins, He is faithful and just to forgive us our sins and to cleanse us from all unrighteousness.

(3) Believe that Jesus is the Son of God, that He died for your sins, and that He rose from the dead.

John 3:16
"For God so loved the world that He gave His only begotten Son, that whoever believes in Him should not perish but have everlasting life."

Romans 10:9 (NIV)
...if you confess with your mouth, "Jesus is Lord," and believe in your heart that God raised him from the dead, you will be saved.

(4) Receive Jesus as your Savior and Lord.

John 1:12
But as many as received Him, to them He gave the right to become children of God, to those who believe in His name.

Romans 10:13
For "whoever calls on the name of the LORD shall be saved."

Suggested Prayer for Salvation

Father, I admit that I have sinned. I ask you to forgive me for every sin I have committed. I believe that Jesus is your Son, and that He died on the cross for my sins and was raised from the dead. I now receive and confess Jesus as my personal Savior and Lord.

Lord Jesus, thank you for dying for me. Come into my heart, and make me the person you want me to be. Amen.

HOW TO RECEIVE THE BAPTISM IN THE HOLY SPIRIT

There is no automatic formula for receiving Holy Spirit baptism. As we have seen in the book of Acts, every time the Holy Spirit was poured out upon individuals, it was a unique experience. Obviously those early believers had no "how to" manuals or handouts on how to receive the baptism in the Holy Spirit.

In the book of Acts, we see two ways that believers are baptized in the Holy Spirit:

(1) By a Sovereign Act of God
(Acts 2:2-4; 10:44-46)

(2) By the Laying On of Hands
(Acts 8:14-17; 19:1-7)

With this in mind, the following guidelines may help and encourage those seeking to receive the Promise of the Father.

Let us emphasize that we are not seeking an experience, but a Person. We desire to be immersed in God, so that His power will be displayed through us for His glory.

Since Jesus is the Baptizer in the Holy Spirit, you can pray to Him anywhere, anytime that you feel ready to receive. Some find it helpful to have a Spirit-filled believer lay hands on them during the impartation.

Receiving the Baptism in the Holy Spirit

The following guidelines are not only for those seeking to receive the Holy Spirit for themselves, but also for those praying for others to receive:

(1) Make sure that you have accepted Jesus Christ as your personal Lord and Savior.

(2) Repent of any known sin.

Admit and turn from your sin, asking God to forgive you. Receiving His forgiveness enables you to approach Him with confidence.

(3) Renounce any association with Satan's kingdom.

We urge anyone who has knowingly or even unknowingly been involved with satanic activity of any kind to repent and renounce his association with Satan's kingdom. Such activities may include reading horoscopes or tarot cards, dabbling in fortune telling or palm reading, playing with Ouija boards, etc.

Ask God to forgive you in the name of Jesus, and to cleanse you with His blood. Declare that you will have no further involvement with any satanic things. A brief, sincere prayer will prepare your heart for the Holy Spirit of God.

(4) Ask Jesus to baptize you.

Since Jesus is the Baptizer, ask Him out loud, in your own words, to baptize you with His Holy Spirit.

(5) Believe that you receive the moment you ask.

(6) Confess that you are receiving the power of the Holy Spirit.

Declare out loud that you are now receiving the baptism in the Holy Spirit and start thanking and praising God for giving Him to you. You can lift your hands, if you like, as a sign of surrender and also of praise.

Usually at this point one becomes aware of the presence of the Holy Spirit. There is a release from within, and the spirit of man springs up to respond to the Spirit of God.

(7) Yield to the Lord and begin to speak in tongues.

By faith switch over from speaking in your known language to speaking in tongues. As the Spirit of God touches you, your own words are no longer adequate to thank and praise God. As the Spirit descends upon you, your speech organs (tongue, lips, vocal chords, etc.) are quickened, producing new syllables and unknown words.

Remember that the Holy Spirit is not speaking in tongues—**you** are. You speak from your heart, but it is not just you. Once you start making new sounds, the Holy Spirit will be with you to give you the words.

It is important during the initial experience that you speak out loud, and not just whisper. Speaking out loud brings about a greater release. On the day of Pentecost, the crowd heard the 120 praising God out loud (Acts 2:11).

The thought might come to you (as it has to hundreds of others): "Oh, that's just me!" Of course it is you. But it's not **just** you. The Holy Spirit is not the one speaking. He is the Helper who prompts and guides, but He does not force anyone to speak.

If you only get a few words, continue to say those words, and before long your heavenly language will be spontaneous and fluent.

(8) Resist any fear or doubt.

Satan is the thief and the liar who wants to steal this precious gift from us by putting fear or doubt into our hearts. Jesus reassured us that if we ask, we will receive (Luke 11:9-10), so do not doubt. Be assured that the heavenly Father is eager to empower you with His Holy Spirit (verse 13).

(9) Don't be disappointed if you don't feel released right away.

You should not focus on the manifestations or feelings. Focus on the Lord. Believe that since you asked in faith, you have received. If you are not released right away in your heavenly language, don't go away feeling defeated. Sometimes people are not released until later. Keep on seeking the Lord, and don't let the enemy discourage you.

(10) Guard your heart against pride.

Avoid the temptation to think that receiving the Holy Spirit and speaking in tongues will make you holier than others. You cannot make yourself more holy or more worthy than the blood of Jesus has already made you.

However, by receiving the power of the Holy Spirit, you are entering into a new dimension of your Christian walk. Remember that this is a new beginning; it is not a graduation or an end in itself. God wants us to continue to grow spiritually and become mature, growing more and more into the image of Christ (Ephesians 4:13).

Suggested Prayer for the Baptism in the Holy Spirit

Dear heavenly Father, thank you for the promise of the Holy Spirit. I believe that this promise is for me. Right now, I repent of all known sins and I renounce all my associations with Satan and his kingdom. I receive your forgiveness and cleansing through the blood of Jesus.

Lord Jesus, I confess you as my Savior and as my Baptizer in the Holy Spirit. I ask you to baptize me in the Holy Spirit, with the evidence of speaking in tongues. Right now, by faith, I receive the Holy Spirit and His power. I surrender my speech organs, and I ask you to give me a pure and holy prayer language. Thank you for the Holy Spirit and His power. Thank you for my new prayer language. I set my heart to walk honorably before you and to be a positive witness to your honor and glory. In your name, Lord Jesus. Amen.

Made in the USA
Las Vegas, NV
31 March 2022